CW00370167

Advanced Guide to Windows XP

Books Available

By the same authors:

If you would like to purchase a Companion Disc for any of the listed books by the same authors, apart from the ones marked with an asterisk, containing the file/program listings which appear in them, then fill in the form at the back of the book and send it to Phil Oliver at the stipulated address.

Advanced Guide to Windows XP

by

N. Kantaris
and
P.R.M. Oliver

Bernard Babani (publishing) Ltd
The Grampians
Shepherds Bush Road
London W6 7NF
England
www.babanibooks.com

Please Note

Although every care has been taken with the production of this book to ensure that any projects, designs, modifications and/or programs, etc., contained herewith, operate in a correct and safe manner and also that any components specified are normally available in Great Britain, the Publishers and Author(s) do not accept responsibility in any way for the failure (including fault in design) of any project, design, modification or program to work correctly or to cause damage to any equipment that it may be connected to or used in conjunction with, or in respect of any other damage or injury that may be so caused, nor do the Publishers accept responsibility in any way for the failure to obtain specified components.

Notice is also given that if equipment that is still under warranty is modified in any way or used or connected with home-built equipment then that warranty may be void.

First Published - October 2004
Reprinted - February 2005
Reprinted - May 2006

British Library Cataloguing in Publication Data:

A catalogue record for this book is available from the British Library

ISBN 0 85934 550 5

Cover Design by Gregor Arthur
Printed and Bound in Great Britain by Cox & Wyman Ltd, Reading

About this Book

Advanced Guide to Windows XP was written to help users to come to grips with some of the more advanced areas of this Operating System. The book covers both the Professional and Home editions of Windows XP (Service Packs 1 and 2).

We start this book by discussing ways to Customise your Windows environment, then look at a possible structure of your data, how to keep your data safe, the filing system, how to look after your hard disc, and how to keep your PC healthy, before embarking on more advanced subjects such as Internet Connections, Network Connections, the Registry, and Scripting.

In this book we assume that Windows XP has been installed on your computer and is up and running. If you need information on such important topics as how to upgrade, what system preparation to make before installing Windows XP, what the hardware requirements are, or which file system to select (FAT32 or NTFS), then may we suggest you refer to our other book *Windows XP explained* (BP514) also published by Bernard Babani (publishing) Ltd.

As with all our other books, this book was written with the busy person in mind. You don't need to read many hundreds of large format pages to find out most of what there is to know about the subject, when fewer pages with illustrated examples can get you going quite adequately!

It is hoped that with the help of this book, you will be able to get the most out of your computer, when using Windows XP, in terms of efficiency and productivity, and that you will be able to do it in the shortest, most effective and enjoyable way.

The book is rounded off with a fairly detailed glossary of terms which should be used with the text of the book when necessary. We also include some selected information in Chapter 12 of material we often found ourselves needing to refer to.

Finally, we hope you have as much fun reading this book as we had writing it. Enjoy!

About the Authors

Noel Kantaris graduated in Electrical Engineering at Bristol University and after spending three years in the Electronics Industry in London, took up a Tutorship in Physics at the University of Queensland. Research interests in Ionospheric Physics, led to the degrees of M.E. in Electronics and Ph.D. in Physics. On return to the UK, he took up a Post-Doctoral Research Fellowship in Radio Physics at the University of Leicester, and then a lecturing position in Engineering at the Camborne School of Mines, Cornwall, (part of Exeter University), where he was also the CSM Computing Manager. At present he is IT Director of FFC Ltd.

Phil Oliver graduated in Mining Engineering at Camborne School of Mines and has specialised in most aspects of surface mining technology, with a particular emphasis on computer related techniques. He has worked in Guyana, Canada, several Middle Eastern and Central Asian countries, South Africa and the United Kingdom, on such diverse projects as: the planning and management of bauxite, iron, gold and coal mines; rock excavation contracting in the UK; international mining equipment sales and international mine consulting. He later took up a lecturing position at Camborne School of Mines (part of Exeter University) in Surface Mining and Management. He has now retired, to spend more time writing, consulting, and developing Web sites.

Acknowledgements

We would like to thank friends and colleagues, for their helpful tips and suggestions which assisted us in the writing of this book.

Trademarks

HP and LaserJet are registered trademarks of Hewlett Packard Corporation.

IBM is a registered trademark of International Business Machines, Inc.

Intel is a registered trademark of Intel Corporation.

Microsoft, **MS-DOS**, **Windows**, are either registered trademarks or trademarks of Microsoft Corporation.

PostScript is a registered trademark of Adobe Systems Incorporated.

All other brand and product names used in the book are recognised as trademarks, or registered trademarks, of their respective companies.

The Windows XP Background

The early versions of Windows ran on top of the MS-DOS (Microsoft's Disc Operating System), and as such were not very stable, were prone to crashing frequently, and had limited support for networking and none at all for multiple user accounts. However, in 1992 Microsoft released Windows for Workgroups 3.1 which allowed the control of small networked groups of computers, followed in late 1993 with version 3.11 which included 32-bit file management and more networking support.

In 1995 Microsoft released Windows 95 (the first 32-bit operating system), followed in 1998 by Windows 98, a much needed upgrade to Windows 95, which ran faster, crashed less often, and supported a host of new technologies. In mid-1999 Windows 98 Second Edition was released. In late 2000, Microsoft released Windows Me, as the direct upgrade to Windows 95/98 for the home PC. Windows Me loaded faster, ran more reliably, and if things went radically wrong through user interference, could be made to return to a previous working version of the Operating System.

Running parallel with the desktop Windows development, Microsoft set up the Windows NT development team with the mission to design and build a PC operating system, primarily for the business server community. From the beginning, the priority design objectives of Windows NT were robustness and extensibility, and in mid-1993 Windows NT 3.1 was released.

Then, in mid-1995 Windows NT 3.51 followed which was capable of supporting upcoming Windows 95 programs, and in mid-1996 Windows NT 4.0 was released. Since then, Windows NT 4.0 has changed a lot, as customer requirements evolved to include support for Windows applications, Web services, communications, and much more. These improvements came in the guise of several Service Packs.

In early 2000, Microsoft released Windows 2000 Professional, together with two additional Windows NT compatible versions of the software; Server and Advanced Server. Users of Windows 95/98 could easily upgrade to the Windows 2000 Professional version of this Operating System, while users of Windows NT could upgrade to one of the other two versions of the Operating System according to their requirements.

Finally, in late 2001, Microsoft released Windows XP (XP for eXPerience) which, however, is known internally to the machine as Windows NT 5.1 - type **ver** at a Command Prompt line to see this for yourself. Windows XP comes in two flavours; the Home edition as the direct upgrade to Windows 98/Me for home users and the Professional edition (with additional functionality) for Windows 2000 or business users. Nevertheless, users of either Windows 98/Me/2000 can choose to upgrade to whichever versions of Windows XP they prefer.

Windows XP has many improvements incorporated into it which fall into several general categories. These are:

- Added features that make Windows XP load faster than any previous version of Windows, run more reliably, and the ability to return to a previous working version of the Operating System (similar to that under Windows Me).

- Improved Wizards (similar to those under Windows Me) let you set up home networks a lot easier and give you the ability to share Internet connections.

- Improved support for digital cameras, video recorders, and multimedia with an improved version of the Windows Media Player (now version 9).

- Improved features and tools in Internet Explorer 6 allow faster performance, and better Web communication from e-mail to instant messaging to video conferencing.

- Improved Windows File Protection (similar to that under Windows 2000) which prevents the replacement of protected system files such as **.sys**, **.dll**, **.ocx**, **.ttf**, **.fon**, and **.exe** files, so that installing software does not corrupt the operating system by overwriting shared system files such as dynamic-link libraries (**.dll** files) and executable files (**.exe** files).

- Windows XP Professional also includes features for power users, such as enhanced file security, remote access to your computer's desktop and a personal Web server.

Most home PC users will find, no doubt, that Windows XP Home Edition contains all the facilities they will ever need or want. Which version you choose will ultimately be your prerogative with the price differential maybe the main factor to be taken into account.

Since the release of Windows XP in 2001, there have been two major updates. The first one was Service Pack 1 (SP1) which contained updates for the following areas of Windows functionality.

- Security issues, including the Windows XP Update Package.

- Operating System reliability.

- Application compatibility.

- Improved Windows XP Setup.

This update and the subsequent release of Service Pack 1a (SP1a) ensured that the Windows XP platform was compatible with new releases of software and hardware, and included updates that resolved issues discovered by customers or by Microsoft's internal testing team.

These updates were made available in the form of downloads from Microsoft or on CD for a small fee.

In August 2004, Microsoft released the second major update to Windows XP, Service Pack 2 (SP2). This update focuses mainly on the security of your computer, and is over 260 MB in size, so downloading it might take a rather long time, particularly if this is done via a 56k modem. Alternatively, you might be able to find a PC magazine that provides this update free on CD.

Whichever way you choose to get this update, we recommend you install it, but ensure that all other programs are closed and that you have made a backup of your data before you start. Installation is extremely easy; just follow the instructions on the screen.

During installation, Setup inspects your current configuration, archives your current files and updates them. This includes making an inventory of your computer's drivers, backing up its registry, creating a restore point, installing the new update files, updating the registry keys, and running various processes. Finally, Setup performs a cleanup and you are asked to restart your PC. The whole installation process takes a good half hour.

Microsoft has made security the central theme of SP2, although there are some additional features that are not specifically geared to protecting your computer. The main visible changes are to be seen in the form of additional Control Panel utilities which allow you to:

- Automatically update windows XP by periodically checking its servers for new updates. These can be downloaded and installed automatically, or you could be notified of their existence so that you could do so at your convenience. This utility makes sure that you do not forget to update your Operating System and thus become compromised by virus attacks.

- Start a new, friendlier, Network Setup Wizard. The Alerter and Messenger services (which were abused by spammers, and annoyed users) are disabled by default. Bluetooth support is now native, which makes communication with suitably equipped PDAs and mobile phones a lot easier.

- Access a new Security Centre which monitors your PC's security settings with respect to its Firewall, Automatic Updates, and Virus protection. If your virus suite cannot be detected or its renewal date is pending, then the Security Centre will let you know.

- Access and configure the new Windows firewall which is far more sophisticated than the old and rather weak Internet Connection Firewall.

- Access a new Wireless Connection Wizard that simplifies the process of joining a wireless service with encryption in place so that your data are protected.

- Outlook Express now includes the Attachment Execution Service which checks the safety of attachments in an effort to unify the approach to attachment security with that of Microsoft Outlook. Now, SP2 protects areas of memory where previously viruses could hide and execute without your knowledge.

Taking everything into consideration, obtaining and installing Service Pack 2 is well worth the effort, and we strongly recommended it.

Note: Although we have installed Windows XP Service Pack 2, the book is also valid for users with Service Pack 1, or indeed for those who have not updated their Operating System at all. The only difference you might notice occasionally, is that a minority of screen dumps might not be exactly the same if you have not installed the latest Windows update but, nevertheless, the points under discussion at the time, which are illustrated by these screen dumps, are not affected. If there is any additional functionality due to the adoption of Service Pack 2, as there is with security issues, then we will bring it to your notice.

Contents

1

Customising Windows XP

Switching on your PC automatically loads Windows XP (or displays the dual-boot option, if you have another Operating System on your hard disc). What displays next depends on which method you have chosen, or was chosen for you for logging on; the Welcome screen (the default), or the Classic screen (similar to the one in Windows 2000). For the moment, we assume that the Welcome screen method is in operation - the one that allows users to log on by simply clicking their icon, as shown in Fig. 1.1 below.

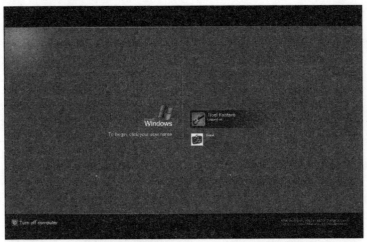

Fig. 1.1 The Windows XP Logon Screen.

Obviously if there are more user accounts on your computer, each user will have their own icon for logging in after the Welcome screen. By default, on installing Windows XP, two accounts are created; the Administrator account, and the Guest account. Other user accounts can be created later (page 131).

The Windows Desktop

In Fig. 1.2, we show the default Windows XP working screen, called the 'Desktop', with the **Recycle Bin** icon displayed on the bottom right of it. In addition, the *start* button at the bottom left corner of the Windows screen has been left-clicked to display the two-column *start* menu. By default the left column provides shortcuts to **Internet Explorer**, **Outlook Express** and the six applications that have been used most often.

On the top of the right-hand column there are shortcuts to such folders as **My Documents**, **My Pictures**, **My Music** and **My Computer**, while on the bottom of the column there are shortcuts to **Control Panel**, **Printers and Faxes**, **Help and Support** and **Search** facility. These might be different for your computer, as they can be changed.

Hovering with the mouse pointer over the **All Programs** button, displays the first column of the cascade menu where all Windows applications are to be found. In Fig. 1.2 below, the System Tools options menu (part of the Windows Accessories) is also shown open.

Fig. 1.2 The Windows XP Start Cascade Menu.

Customising the Start Menu

At the top of the *start* menu the name of the current user is displayed with a picture against it. Left-clicking this picture opens the User Accounts screen shown in Fig. 1.3.

Fig. 1.3 The User Accounts Dialogue Box.

From here you can choose a different picture for the current user either from the ones supplied or from one of your own. You can also change the Computer's theme, desktop, screen savers, etc. Most of these facilities will be discussed shortly.

New to Windows XP is the ability of the first of its two-column menus to adapt to the way you use your computer - an adaptation of what was first introduced with Windows Me. It keeps track of what features and programs you use the most and adds them to the list on the left column. For example, if you use the **Notepad** by selecting from the Accessories sub-menu, next time you click the *start* button you will see this application pinned to the bottom of the first column of the *start* menu. This saves time as you don't have to scroll through menu lists to find the application you want to use.

To remove an application from the first column of the *start* menu, right-click it and select **Remove from this List** as shown in Fig. 1.4 on the next page. This removes the name of the application from the list, not the application itself from your hard disc.

Fig. 1.4 The User Accounts Dialogue Box.

As can be seen, you also have a menu option to **Pin to Start menu** any program. This adds it to the top of the left column of the *start* menu which is a more permanent list.

You can also use this facility to pin your favourite programs, even if these are to be found in the **All Programs** menu, thus customising the way you run your computer and cutting down the endless number of shortcuts that most users seem to place on the desktop.

As seen in Fig. 1.4, the list of programs displayed here differs from those displayed in Fig. 1.2. The reason for this is that Fig. 1.2 displays the default menu options placed there by the Windows Setup program, while the list displayed in Fig. 1.4 is the logged user's choice of programs after lengthy use of the Windows program.

Once you have pinned your chosen programs to the *start* menu, you could rename by right-clicking their entry on the list and selecting **Rename** from the drop-down menu. You could even change their order on the list. To move an item on the *start* menu, point to it to highlight it, then drag it with the right mouse button pressed to the desired position on the list.

The Windows Control Panel

The Control Panel provides a quick and easy way to change the hardware and software settings of your system. To access it, use the *start*, **Control Panel** menu command which opens the Control Panel window shown in Fig. 1.5 below.

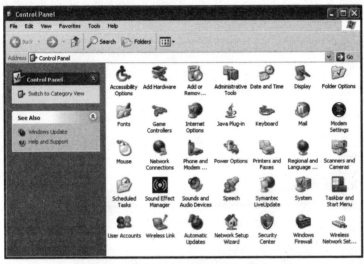

Fig. 1.5 The Control Panel Window.

Double-clicking the Control Panel icons allows you to add new hardware, add or remove programs, change the display type and its resolution, change the printer fonts, and change the keyboard repeat rate. Further, you can change the settings of your mouse, install and configure your printer(s), specify regional settings, such as the formatting of numbers and dates, and access a variety of system administrative tools. If your system is connected to the outside world or supports multimedia, then you can also configure it appropriately.

All of these features control the environment in which the Windows application programs operate and you should become familiar with them. The last 5 icons are added to the Control Panel only after you have installed Service Pack 2, as mentioned in The Windows XP Background section on page xi.

Changing the Display Settings

If your VDU (visual display unit or screen) is capable of higher resolution than the minimum required 800 by 600 pixels (picture elements) by Windows XP, you might like to increase its resolution to, say, 1024 by 768 pixels, or higher (we have used 1440 by 900 for a wide screen PC). This will allow you to see a larger number of icons on a screen when a given application is activated.

To do this, use the *start*, **Control Panel** menu command, and in the Control Panel window (Classic view), double-click the **Display** icon shown here. In the Display Properties dialogue box, click the Settings tab to display the dialogue box shown in Fig. 1.6 with the settings changed appropriately.

For the new settings to take effect, click the **Apply** button followed by the **OK** button to close the dialogue box.

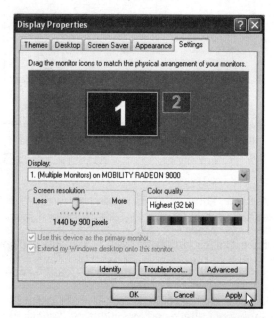

Fig. 1.6 The Settings Screen of the Display Properties Dialogue Box.

While the Display Properties dialogue box is open, you might like to explore the other available settings. For example:

Click the Desktop tab to change the background of your desktop, which by default was set to 'Bliss'. We found the Azul more 'summery' and changed it to that, as shown stretched in Fig. 1.7. Additional Desktop choices can be made available here by adding photos to the **My Pictures** folder.

Fig. 1.7 The Themes Screen of the Display Properties Box.

If you now click the Themes tab you will find that the theme is listed as 'Modified'. Other themes on the list are the Windows Classic which presents you with a display more akin to that of previous versions of Windows, the Windows XP theme which displays the default screen of Fig. 1.2.

Click the Appearance tab to select a different look for your windows and buttons, apply a different colour scheme and select a different font size.

Click the Screen Savers tab to select a different screen saver - you will be able to preview your selection. We chose 'My Pictures Slideshow', as shown in Fig. 1.8, which displays all the pictures in the **My Pictures** folder.

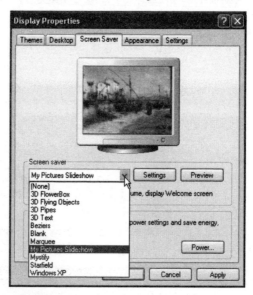

Fig. 1.8 The Screen Saver Choice in the Display Properties Box.

From this screen you can also select power settings which vary according to the type of PC. For example, you can choose from various Power Schemes, set an Alarm and/or display a Power

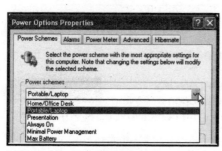

Fig. 1.9 The Themes Screen of the Display Properties Box.

Meter if you are a laptop user, use the Advanced tab screen to select whether to be prompted for your password when the PC resumes from Standby, and whether to Hibernate or not on switching off.

Taskbar Buttons

At the bottom of the Desktop screen is the Taskbar. It contains the *start* button which, as we have seen, can be used to quickly start a program. Later on we will discuss how we can search for a file, and how to get Help.

Fig. 1.10 Quick Launch Activation.

Before we go any further, right-click an empty part of the Taskbar, point to the **Toolbars** option which displays the sub-menu, shown on the left in Fig. 1.10, and left-click the **Quick Launch** entry. This displays three icons next to the *start* button; left-clicking one of these, launches its application (see next page for details).

When you open a program, or a window, a button for it is placed on the Taskbar, as shown in Fig. 1.11 below.

Fig. 1.11 The Windows Taskbar.

You can left-click your mouse on this button to make this the active program, or window, which displays in a darker shade of blue on the Taskbar. So, now you can always see what windows you have open, which is the active one, and quickly switch between them. As more buttons are placed on the Taskbar their size shrinks slightly, but up to a point. After that common entries are grouped together with a number indicating the number of open windows. To see details relating to a grouped button, left-click it to open a list of components, as shown in Fig. 1.12. Try it!

Fig. 1.12 Grouped Taskbar Entries.

Another interesting Taskbar menu option is **Properties** in Fig. 1.10. This allows you to change the Taskbar and *start* menu options, as shown in Fig. 1.13 on the next page.

Fig. 1.13 The Taskbar and Start Menu Properties Box.

If you have activated the Quick Launch option, there will be three buttons displaying next to the *start* button. These, in order of appearance, have the following functions:

Launch the Internet Explorer Browser.

Show Desktop.

Launch Windows Media Player.

Fig. 1.14 Date and Time Properties Dialogue Box.

The Taskbar also shows the current time to the far right, the Windows Messenger, the Options, the Restore and the Language icons. Moving the mouse pointer over the clock will display the date. Double-clicking the clock, opens the Date/Time Properties box, shown in Fig. 1.14, so that you can make changes, if necessary.

Exiting Windows XP

To exit Windows, click the *start* button and select the **Turn Off Computer** option, as shown in Fig. 1.15.

Fig. 1.15 The Lower Part of the Start Menu.

This opens an additional box, shown in Fig. 1.16 below.

Fig. 1.16 The Turn Off Computer Box.

From here you can either put your computer in a **Stand by** mode, **Turn Off** the computer, or **Restart** it. The **Stand by** mode is used to save power by turning off your monitor and/or hard disc after a specified time interval. If you press the **Shift** key down while pointing to the **Stand By** icon, it will change to **Hibernate** (we will discuss these two topics next). Selecting the **Turn Off** option, exits all the open programs, carries out any file saves you require and then tells you when it is safe to switch off your computer. The **Restart** option is used if you want to clear the memory settings and restart Windows XP, or if you have a dual boot system the other operating system.

Note: Unlike previous versions of Windows where this was the only way that you should end a session, with Windows XP you can just switch off your computer - the **Turn Off** the computer procedure will then be carried out automatically.

Standby Mode

When your computer is put into standby mode, information in memory is not saved to your hard disc. You must save all your work before putting your computer into standby mode, because if there is an interruption in power, all information in the computer's memory will be lost.

To control standby mode, activate the Control Panel and click on the Power Options icon. In the displayed Power Options Properties dialogue box, click the Power Schemes tab, as shown in Fig. 1.17.

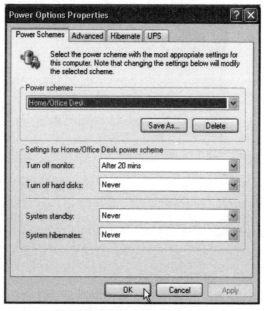

Fig. 1.17 The Power Options Power Scheme Screen.

If you are using a portable computer, you can specify one setting for battery power and a different setting for AC power. In fact, you can adjust any power management option that your computer's hardware configuration supports.

Hibernation Mode

When your computer is put into hibernation mode, everything in the computer memory is saved on your hard disc, and your computer is switched off. When you turn the computer back on, all programs and documents that were open when you turned the computer off are restored on the desktop.

To control hibernation, activate the **Control Panel** and double-click the **Power Options** icon shown here. Then, in the displayed Power Options Properties dialogue box, click the Hibernate tab. If the Hibernate tab is unavailable, then this is because your computer does not support this feature. If it does, make sure the **Enable hibernation** box is checked, as shown in Fig. 1.18.

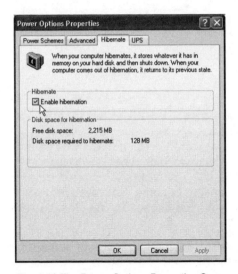

Fig. 1.18 The Power Options Properties Screen.

Next, click the Advance tab and select what you want under **Options**, then click the down-arrow button against the **When I press the power button on my computer** box and choose what you want to happen from the drop-down options list shown in Fig. 1.19.

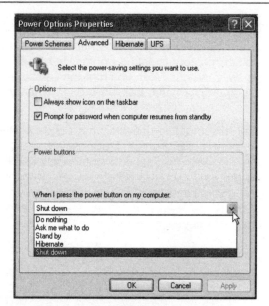

Fig. 1.19 The Power Button Options List.

Next, click the Power Schemes tab, and select a time in **System hibernates**. If you set this to, say, 'after 1 min', then you can sit back and see what happens. With our system, after one minute we were informed that it was safe to switch off the computer, which we did. When switching on the computer a few seconds later, Windows XP started up automatically (the dual boot option became unavailable) and loaded all the programs that happened to be loaded at the time of hibernation.

Occasionally, hibernation causes some programs not to work correctly. If you come across such program misbehaviour, then simply restart Windows which resolves such problems.

If you decide that you do not want your system to hibernate, just go through the procedure described above and remove the check mark from the selected option in the Power Options Properties screen of Fig. 1.18. Finally, click the Power Schemes tab, and select 'never' for the time the **System hibernates**.

Changing the Logon/Logoff Settings

To change the way you log on to your computer, double-click the **User Accounts** icon, shown here, in the **Control Panel**, to display the screen shown in Fig. 1.20.

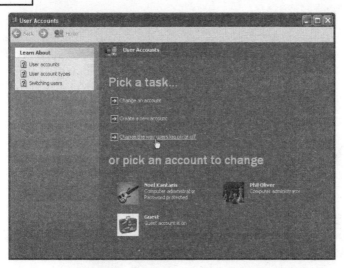

Fig. 1.20 The User Accounts Dialogue Box.

Next, click the **Change the way users log on or off** to display the screen shown in Fig. 1.21 below.

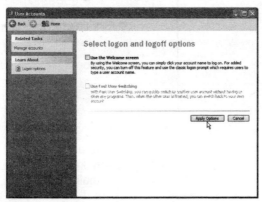

Fig. 1.21 Selecting the Logon and Logoff Options.

In the displayed dialogue box (Fig. 1.21) remove the check mark from the **Use the Welcome screen** box, and click the **Apply Options** button.

Now using the *start*, **Log Off** option and after the display of a confirmation box, Windows logs off the current user and displays the Log On to Windows dialogue box shown in Fig. 1.22. In the **User name** box change the name of the currently logged user to **Administrator**, type in the **Password**, and click **OK**. If you have forgotten this password, please refer to the 'Note' on the penultimate page of Chapter 9.

Fig. 1.22 The Log On to Windows Dialogue Box.

From now on, when you use the *start*, **Shut Down** option, you will be given several different options for shutting down Windows, as shown in Fig. 1.23. The currently logged user appears as the first option.

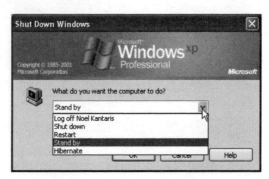

Fig. 1.23 The Shut Down Windows Dialogue Box.

2

Windows Folders and Files

In the right-hand pane of the *start* menu you will find listed the most frequently used folders in Windows, such as **My Documents**, **My Pictures**, and **My Music**. The **My Documents** window is shown open in Fig. 2.1 below.

Fig. 2.1 The Toolbar of a Windows Application.

Fig. 2.2 The View Sub-menu.

To see the display exactly as it appears in Fig. 2.1, you need to click the down arrow against the **Views** button on the Toolbar and select the **List** option from the drop-down menu, as shown above. Try the different display options available to you and see which one you prefer.

Note that the above mentioned windows, as well as the **My Computer**, **My Network Places**, and **Recycle Bin** windows, have a Toolbar with browser-style forwards and backwards arrows similar to the **Internet Explorer** which is bundled with Windows XP.

As you can see from Fig. 2.1, Windows keeps, by default, the **My Pictures**, and **My Music** folders within the **My Documents** folder. In what follows, we will carry on with this structured tradition, so that folders we create are also contained within the **My Documents** folder. In this way, when you left-click **My Documents** on the *start* menu, all the other folders will be available to you.

The above folder structure makes it a lot easier to backup all your valuable data by simply backing up the **My Documents** folder, which will also backup all its sub-folders. It is possible, of course, that you might have a partitioned hard disc (as we do - see Fig. 2.3 - drives C: and D:), or more than one fixed hard disc attached to your system in which you can keep your data. Whether you have such additional discs or not, is not important as the skills required to keep one organised can also be applied to the others.

Fig. 2.3 The My Computer Window.

My Computer

In Windows XP you can work with files using My Computer in two different ways; in the hierarchical structure form, or by using commands in the Tasks pane. Both these methods will be discussed, starting with the Tasks pane view.

As we have seen on the previous page, left-clicking the **My Computer** icon on the *start* menu, gives you immediate visual access to all the disc drives in your computer, as well as **Shared Files** and the logged user's Documents folder. The My Computer window opens with the last settings you selected, and a Web browser type toolbar.

To make the program function in a similar visual manner to Windows Explorer, click the **Folders** icon on its Toolbar. To see all the folders held on your computer's drive, click the appropriate disc icon that holds Windows XP (in our case this is Local Disc C:, yours could be different), as shown in Fig. 2.4.

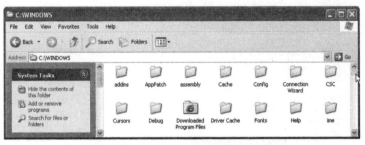

Fig. 2.4 The Contents of the WINDOWS Folder.

Note: If you select to open the WINDOWS folder that holds Windows XP system files, as we have done above, the message 'This folder contains files that keep your system working properly ...' appears in the right pane of the displayed window. Left-clicking the **View the entire contents of this folder** link allows you to have a look. But, as the warning tells you, do not move, delete, or in any way change the content of these folders or files - just look.

To see the same display, but in hierarchical form, use the **View**, **Explorer Bar** menu command and select the **Folders** option, which displays a window similar to the one in Fig. 2.5.

Fig. 2.5 The Contents of the Program Files Folder.

Folders are graphical devices, as shown here, similar to directories in that they can contain files, other folders and also icons. To see a few files in the WINDOWS folder, scroll down past all the folders.

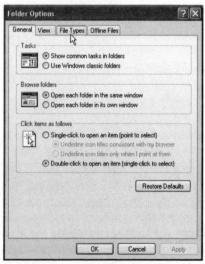

Fig. 2.6 The Folder Options Dialogue Box.

Icon settings are easy to change, not only from the **Views** button on the toolbar, but also from the **View** menu. However, to control general settings, view options and edit the files you view, use the **Tools**, **Folder Options** menu command, which opens the Folder Options dialogue box shown in Fig. 2.6.

To see what program associations are valid on your system, click the File Types tab. This opens the dialogue box shown in Fig. 2.7 on the next page.

If you work your way down the list of **Registered file types** you can see the association details in the lower half of the box. Our example shows that a file with the **.AU** extension is a sound file.

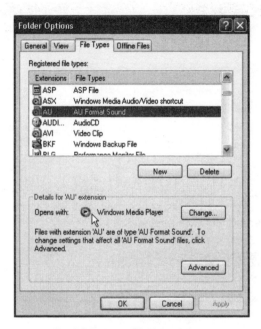

Fig. 2.7 Program File Associations.

From this box you can add new associations by clicking the **New** button, delete them with the **Delete** button and change them with the **Change** button. Without getting too involved at this stage, it is worth spending a few minutes just browsing through the list. It will help you to recognise the icons. These extensions are used by Windows XP to associate files with the application that created them.

Any file displayed within the My Computer window, whether with its extension showing or not, can be opened by double-clicking its icon. If it is a program file, the program will run. If it is a document, it will be opened in a running version of its application program.

Creating and Naming a New Folder

To create a new folder within, say **My Documents**, locate the folder, left-click it to highlight it and either use the **Make a new folder** entry on the **Tasks** pane (see Fig. 2.1), or the **File**, **New** command in the hierarchical view and select **Folder** option, as shown in Fig. 2.8 below.

Fig. 2.8 Creating a New Folder.

When Windows creates a new folder it places it at the end of the list of existing folders and names it **New Folder**, highlighting its name and waiting for you to name it, as shown here to the right.

Next, type a name, say, Photos, which replaces the default name given to it by Windows. If this doesn't happen, it must be because you have clicked the left mouse button an extra time which fixes the default name.

To rename a folder or a file, right-click the folder or file and select the **Rename** option from the drop-down quick menu, then type a different name to replace the existing one.

Searching for Files and Folders

To search for files, left-click the *start* menu and select the **Search** option. This opens the Search Dialogue box, the left panel of which is shown in Fig. 2.9. Next, click the **All files and folders** entry in the Tasks pane (as shown in Fig. 2.9).

You now need to specify the name (or part of it - see next page) of the item you are searching for and the drive you want to search (in this case the drive where Windows is installed on your PC), as shown in Fig. 2.10.

Fig. 2.9 Specifying Type of Search.

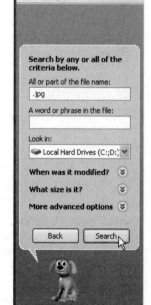

Fig. 2.10 Specifying the Item and Drive for a Search.

Filename Convention

File names can be as long as 255 characters, including spaces, but keeping them short is a very good idea as long names can result in typographical errors. However, the name must not contain any of the following keyboard characters:

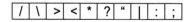

A filename can also include a file extension which is the optional suffix following the period in a filename. Windows uses this to identify the application program that created it. For example, documents created with Microsoft Word have the extension **.doc** added automatically to the saved file. In this way Windows knows that this file was created by Microsoft Word. Double-clicking such a filename causes Windows to load Microsoft Word first then open the letter ready for any changes you might want to make to it.

Below we list some of the popular filename extensions.

.bak	a backup file
.exe	an executable file
.hlp	a hypertext help file
.html	a hypertext markup language file
.jpeg or **.jpg**	a graphic format file
.rtf	a rich text format file
.sys	a system file
.tmp or **.temp**	a temporary file
.txt	a basic text file
.wav	a waveform of a soundbite.

File Properties

To find out more about a particular file, right-click it and select **Properties** from the drop-down menu to open the Properties dialogue box, as shown in Fig. 2.11. Here, the full properties of the file are listed, including its name, type, location, size, etc. You can also change the file's attributes, by making it, say, **Read-only**, to prevent accidental changes to its contents. The Properties dialogue box of some types of files has an extra tab which allows you to preview, or even play, their contents.

Fig. 2.11 The Properties Box.

Sending Folders and Files

A very useful feature of Windows is the ability to quickly send files and folders to specific destinations.

Fig. 2.12 Sending Folders and Files.

Right-clicking selected folders, or files, will open the menu shown in Fig. 2.12. Selecting the **Send To** option opens the list of available destinations. In your case these are bound to be different, for example, DVD-RW Drive (E:) option might not be available to you.

Selecting the **3½ Floppy (A:)** option will copy any selected folders and files to a removable disc in the (A:) drive, as shown in Fig. 2.13 by the very decorative animated window that appears while the process is being carried out.

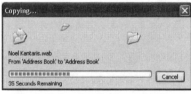

Fig. 2.13 Copying Folders and Files.

It is easy to add more locations to the **Send To** menu, as it is controlled by the contents of the SendTo folder, which is itself in the Windows folder. However, the SendTo folder is hidden by default, so if you use the *start,* **Search** command, you may not find it. To make it visible, start **My Computer**, then use the **Tools, Folder Options** command, click the View tab and finally click the **Show hidden files and folders** option.

To add a destination to the **Send To** menu, click the Documents and Settings folder on the drive where Windows XP is installed, then double-click the folder of a specific user. Next, double-click the SendTo folder, use the **File, New, Shortcut** command, and follow the instructions on your screen. One useful application to add to the SendTo folder is Notepad so that you can send text files to it, to see and maybe edit them.

Deleting Folders and Files

To delete or remove folders or files, first highlight them, and then either select the **Delete the selected items** entry in the Tasks pane, press the **Del** key on the keyboard, or press the **Delete** button on the Toolbar, shown here, or use the **File**, **Delete** command from the window menu bar. All of these methods open the confirmation box which gives you the chance to abort the operation by selecting **No**. Deleted folders or files are sent to the Recycle Bin.

The Recycle Bin

To open the Recycle Bin, double-click its desktop icon, shown here. The Recycle Bin window lists all the files, folders, icons and shortcuts that have been deleted from fixed drives since it was last emptied, as shown in Fig. 2.14.

Fig. 2.14 The Recycle Bin Window.

Note: Windows keeps a record of the original locations of the deleted items, so that it can restore them if necessary. To restore specific files or folders from the Recycle Bin, first select them then use the appropriate Tasks pane entry which changes from the above to **Restore the selected items** (in the hierarchical view, you will need to use the **File** sub-menu). This will restore the selected files to the folder they were originally in, even if you have deleted that folder. Pressing the **Del** keyboard button, removes the selected items from the Recycle Bin.

To save disc space, every now and then, open the Recycle Bin and delete unwanted folders or files. To delete all the files and folders held in the Recycle Bin, click the **Empty the Recycle Bin** entry in the Tasks pane.

Other Views in My Computer

It is perhaps worth looking at some additional views in **My Computer** which greatly enhance its functionality. These are to be found mainly in the **View**, **Explorer Bar** menu options shown in Fig. 2.15.

The Search View

Use this to display the **Search** facility in the left pane of a **My Computer** window which is identical in functionality to the *start*, **Search** command.

The Favorites View

Use this to display a list of favourite links in the left pane of **My Computer** window (Fig. 2.16). It allows you to add and organise useful URL addresses, or access various pre-set media addresses on the Internet. To display the same list left-click the Favorites entry in the **My Computer** menu bar.

Fig. 2.15 The Explorer Bar Options.

The Media View

Use this to be connected to the Internet (provided you have this facility) and display the Web site WindowsMedia.com in the left pane of **My Computer**, as shown in Fig. 2.17.

Fig. 2.16 The Favorites Pane.

In this window click the Media Options down arrow at the bottom of the screen to select which media you want to connect to. For example, selecting **Radio Guide** displays a full screen in the right pane of **My Computer** window, as shown below.

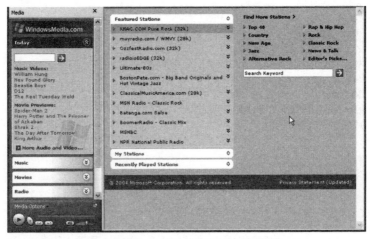

Fig. 2.17 The WindowsMedia.com Web Site.

If you are not connected to the Internet, you can work off-line with files in **My Music** or **My Videos** folder, as shown in Fig. 2.18, by clicking the **Go back to the previous menu** link on the displayed left pane of the screen.

Selecting one of the radio stations and clicking the **Play** button connects you to it and opens up a separate Internet Explorer window and the Media Player to display information about the station and provide a visual accompaniment to the music.

Fig. 2.18 The Media Window.

However, unless you have a Broadband connection to the Internet, you will experience reception delays due to buffering which is the process of sending a certain amount of information to the computer before the content actually plays.

The History View

Use this to display the **History** facility in the left pane of My Computer window. It allows you to see which 'pages' were visited recently , as shown in Fig. 2.19. It includes files and folders on your system, other computers connected to your system or sites on the Internet. You can select to see today's history or that of other periods as shown at the top of the display.

Fig. 2.19 The History Pane.

The Folders View

As we saw earlier (see page 20), clicking this option in the **View**, **Explorer Bar** menu, displays a hierarchical 'system tree' on the left panel of **My Computer** window showing all the resources of your computer (see Fig. 2.5), as well as those of a network you might be connected to.

The system tree lists Objects which contain sub-folders with a plus sign (+). Clicking a (+) sign, opens it up to reveal the sub-folders beneath. When sub-folders are displayed, the (+) sign changes to a minus sign (–), indicating that the parent folder can be collapsed. This is shown in the example on page 20, Fig. 2.5, where the **Program Files** folder in the C: drive is expanded.

The right-hand, or contents, pane is automatically displayed when you select a folder from the tree. As with most Windows XP system windows, you can change the format of the information shown in the contents pane by clicking the Views button on the Toolbar and selecting an appropriate option from the drop-down menu.

The Picture and Fax Viewer

New to Windows XP is the Picture and Fax Viewer. You can use it to view, rotate, and perform basic tasks with all kinds of image documents, including scanned pictures, downloaded pictures from a digital camera, and fax documents, without opening an image editing program. Such images can be viewed as thumbnails or in a filmstrip, and fax documents can be annotated.

To open the Picture and Fax Viewer, locate the picture you want to view and double-click its filename. This displays your picture in the Viewer, for us the stormy sea shown in Fig. 2.20 below.

Fig. 2.20 The Windows Picture and Fax Viewer.

Note the buttons at the bottom of the screen. You can use these to navigate through your pictures folder, select the viewing size, view the pictures in your folder as a slide show, zoom in or out, rotate the image, and generally carry out certain housekeeping functions, including the opening of the picture in Microsoft Photo Editor so that you can edit it. The precise function of these buttons is described in Fig. 2.21.

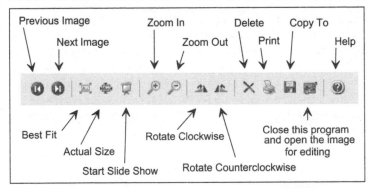

Fig. 2.21 The Windows Picture and Fax Viewer Toolbar.

Clicking the **Close this program and open the image for editing** button on the Windows **Picture and Fax Viewer** Toolbar, displays the selected image ready for you to edit it.

The My Pictures Folder

In Fig. 2.22 below, we demonstrate some of these features by displaying the **My Pictures** folder in **My Computer** as Thumbnails. The other available viewing facilities are seen in the **View** menu which is also open.

Fig. 2.22 A Pictures Folder Displayed in Thumbnail View.

Icons can be arranged by name, size, type, etc., from the **View** menu, or can be previewed, rotated, set as desktop background, or opened in a variety of imaging programs, from a shortcut (right-click) menu, as shown in Fig. 2.23 below.

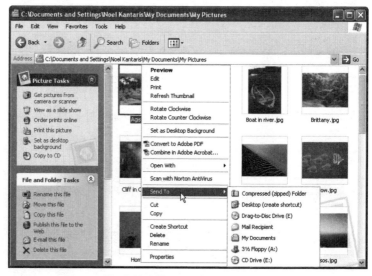

Fig. 2.23 A Picture's Shortcut Menu.

You can use this drop-down menu or the **Pictures Tasks** menu, to select from a variety of options. For example, you can view pictures as a slide show, set a selected picture as a desktop background, print a selected picture, or copy selected pictures to a CD. You can also carry out all the other functions listed under the **File and Folder Tasks**.

One very useful facility is using the **E-mail this file** link from the **File and Folder Tasks** menu. The same can be done from the right-click **Send To** menu by selecting the **Mail Recipient** option. Either of these options give you the choice to 'make your pictures smaller' which automatically compresses pictures to around 50 KB and automatically attaches them to a blank e-mail, ready for you to type a few words before sending it.

To see your pictures in another interesting display, use the **View**, **Filmstrip** command. To get the full benefit of this view, you need to increase the size of the displayed window to at least ¾ of the size of your screen. The result should look similar to that in Fig. 2.24.

Fig. 2.24 Pictures Displayed in Filmstrip View.

As each picture is selected, an enlarged view of it displays above the filmstrip. The four buttons below the enlarged view can be used to navigate to the previous or the next image, and to rotate the selected picture clockwise or anticlockwise.

Note: If there are several people using the same computer, then each person's **My Pictures** folder is located in the drive where Windows XP was installed (ours is in drive C:) as a sub-folder to:

`C:\Documents and Settings\User name\My Documents\My Pictures`

If the folder is a shared folder then it will be found in:

`C:\Documents and Settings\All Users\Documents\My Pictures`

Copying Files and Folders to a CD

New to Windows XP is the ability to copy files and folders to a CD. You will need a recordable compact disc (CD-R) or a rewritable compact disc (CD-RW) and a CD recorder.

To start the process, insert a blank recordable or rewritable CD in the CD recorder, open **My Computer** and select the files or folders you want to copy to the CD. Make sure that the selected files and folders do not exceed the CD's capacity (normally 650 MB for a standard CD).

You can either use the **Copy to CD** option under the **Picture Tasks** on the left pane of **My Computer**, or right-click your selected pictures, choose the **Send To** entry from the drop-down menu, and click the **CD Drive** option (see Fig. 2.23).

Either action displays the message shown in Fig. 2.25 on the right end of the Taskbar.

Fig. 2.25 Message on Taskbar.

To see the files, which are held in a temporary area, before they are copied to the CD, click the message balloon to display a screen similar to that in Fig. 2.26.

Fig. 2.26 Files in Temporary Area Awaiting to be Burned onto a CD.

Now is the time to perhaps exclude some of these files (by deleting them) before clicking the **Write these files to CD** entry under the CD Writing Tasks panel.

Compressing Files and Folders

Compressing files and folders allows you to greatly increase the storage capacity of your discs with no extra hardware cost. To use this much improved option in Windows XP, select the file(s) and or folder which you want to compress in **My Computer**, then right-click it and choose the **Send To** followed by the **Compressed (zipped) Folder** options from the drop-down menu shown in Fig. 2.27 below.

Fig. 2.27 Sending a File to a Zipped Folder.

After momentarily displaying an information box to let you know the action being carried out, Windows creates a new folder which has the extension **.zip,** inside which you will find your compressed file. Should you rename this zipped folder, you must retain the **.zip** extension.

You can add other files and folders to a compressed folder by dragging them onto it. Selected files are then compressed one at time before they are moved into the folder, while the contents of the dragged folders are also compressed.

To find out the size (before and after compression) of an individual file which might be one of many inside a zipped folder, double-click the compressed folder to display its contents, then right-click the required file and select **Properties** from the drop-down menu to display a box similar to the one shown in Fig. 2.28 below.

Fig. 2.28 Compressed File Properties.

As you can see, compressing the present chapter of this book has reduced its size from nearly 11 MB to nearly 4 MB - quite a saving on disc space.

You can open files and programs in a compressed folder by double-clicking them. If a program requires **.dll** (dynamic link library) or data files to run, then those files must first be extracted. To extract compressed files and folders from a zipped folder, either right-click the compressed folder and select the **Extract All** option from the drop-down menu, or open the compressed folder by double-clicking it, then select **Extract all files** under the **Folder Tasks**.

This starts the **Extraction Wizard** in which you can specify where you want these files and folders to be extracted to. When you extract a file or folder it leaves a copy of it in the zipped folder.

Moving Files and Settings

If you are running Windows XP on a new computer and you want to move your data files and personal settings from your old computer to the new one, without having to go through the same configuration you did with your old computer, then you need to use the **Files and Settings Transfer Wizard**.

The Wizard can help you easily and quickly move your personal display properties, Taskbar and Folder options, and Internet browser and e-mail settings from your old computer and place them on the new one. Other folders and files that are also moved are **My Documents**, **My Pictures**, and **Favorites**. The transfer can be carried out either by a direct cable connection between the two computers, via a floppy drive or other removable media, or a network drive.

To start the process, you will need to run the **Files and Settings Transfer Wizard** on both your old and new machine. To do this on your old machine, place the Windows XP distribution CD in its CD-ROM drive and on the first installation screen click the **Perform additional tasks** option to open the screen in Fig. 2.29.

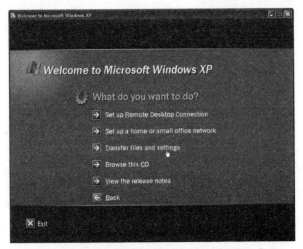

Fig. 2.29 Selecting the Transfer Files and Settings Option
from the Windows XP Distribution CD.

On that screen, click the **Transfer files and settings** option to start the Wizard on your old machine.

To open the **Files and Settings Transfer Wizard** on your new machine, use the *start*, **All Programs**, **Accessories**, **System Tools** command, then click the **Files and Settings Transfer Wizard** option. This opens the first screen of the Wizard, as shown in Fig. 2.30.

Fig. 2.30 The Files and Settings Transfer Wizard.

In subsequent Wizard screens, on both machines, you are told:

- To state whether this is your new or old computer.

- To state which media you want to use for the creation of a Wizard disc which will contain all your relevant files and settings.

- To specify which files and folders you want to transfer. Don't go overboard with your selection here as it could take a very long time to accomplish the task.

- To finish, go to the new computer with the newly created disc, start the Wizard and complete the transfer.

3

Controlling Peripherals

In this chapter we will examine how you can change your PC's settings for printers, keyboard, mouse, modem, scanner and camera. We begin by using the *start*, **Control Panel** menu command which (in the Classic view) displays the screen in Fig. 3.1 below. From here you can control all your peripherals.

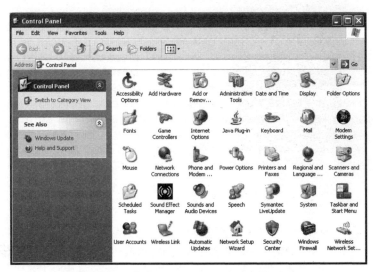

Fig. 3.1 The Control Panel Screen in Classic View.

Printers and Faxes

Double-clicking the **Printers and Faxes** icon, shown here, displays the screen in Fig. 3.2 on the next page. From here, you can add a printer, add a fax printer, or check their configuration.

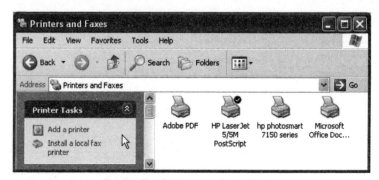

Fig. 3.2 The Printers and Faxes Folder.

Nearly 1,000 different printers are supported by Windows XP so, hopefully, you shouldn't have too much trouble getting yours to work. The printer and printing functions are included in a single Printers and Faxes folder, which you can also open by clicking its entry, shown to the left, in the *start* menu. Our Printers and Faxes folder, shown in Fig. 3.2 above, has several printers available for use, and a list of **Printer Tasks**. Items in this list provide an easy way of adding new printers, installing a local fax printer, and when a printer is selected entries are added to configure existing ones, and manage all your print jobs.

Windows XP, just like previous versions of Windows, supports the following printer set-up methods:

* Plug and Play printers are automatically detected at installation time, or during the boot-up process. You will be prompted for the necessary driver files if they are not already in the Windows directory, these should be supplied with a new Plug-and-Play printer.

* Point and Print printing enables you to quickly connect to, and use, printers shared on some other networked PCs.

* For other situations, the **Add Printer Wizard** steps you through the printer installation process, whether the new printer is connected to your PC, or on a network.

Adding a Printer

Installing an additional printer (not connected to your system, but available to you, say, at work) allows you to use the additional fonts available to this printer (we will discuss fonts shortly). Below we will step through the procedure of installing such a printer to your system.

To start installation, click the **Add a Printer** entry in the **Printer Tasks** list of the Printers and Faxes window, shown in Fig. 3.2. This opens the **Add Printers Wizard**, which makes the installation procedure very easy indeed. As with all Wizards, you progress from screen to screen by clicking the **Next** button. In the second Wizard screen, shown in Fig. 3.3, click the **Local printer attached to this computer** option if this is the case and the printer is connected to your computer.

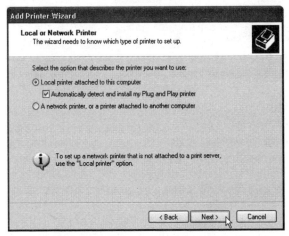

Fig. 3.3 The Second Screen of the Add Printer Wizard.

The first time you activate the **Add Printer Wizard**, and after pressing the **Next** button on the screen of Fig. 3.3, the Wizard scans your computer for installed Plug and Play printers and updates its built-in database. If it doesn't find one, it assumes that you want to install a printer manually and asks you to click **Next** to proceed.

On the next Wizard screen choose FILE: as the port you want to use with the printer and select it from the displayed extensive list, as shown in Fig. 3.4. If your printer is not on the list, then either use the disc provided by the manufacturer of your printer, or go to the Internet for an update on the list of printers.

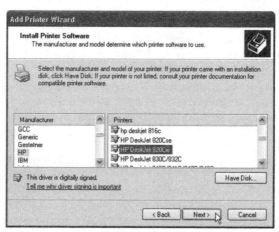

Fig. 3.4 Using the Wizard to Manually Select a Printer.

Documents prepared with this printer selection, can then be printed to file on, say a 3½" floppy disc, or a re-writable CD disc, and later printed out on the selected printer (even if it is not connected to your computer and does not itself have access to the particular application you are using). Later you can copy that file to the selected printer from its attached PC by issuing the simple command

```
COPY A:\Filename LPT1: /B
```

The /B switch in this command tells the printer to expect a binary file (with embedded printer codes).

Note that the PC which is connected to the additional printer does not even have to operate under Windows for you to print your work, as the command is given at the Command prompt. If the PC does operate under Windows XP, you will need to use the *start*, **All Programs**, **Accessories**, **Command Prompt** command, then issue the COPY command.

Configuring your Printer

All configuration for a printer is consolidated onto a tabbed

Fig. 3.5 The Object Menu.

property sheet that is accessed from its icon in the Printers and Faxes folder. Right-clicking a printer icon opens the object menu, shown in Fig. 3.5, which gives control of the printer's operation.

As a newly installed printer is automatically set as the default printer, you might want to change this by selecting the printer connected to your PC and clicking the **Set as Default Printer** option on the object menu. If you click the **Properties** option, the window shown in Fig. 3.6

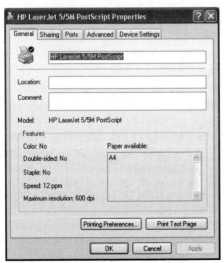

Fig. 3.6 The Printer Properties Window.

opens and lets you control all the printer's parameters, such as the printer port (or network path), paper and graphics options, built-in fonts, and other device options specific to the printer model. All these settings are fairly self explanatory and as they depend on your printer type, we will let you work them out for yourself.

Once you have installed and configured your printers in Windows they are then available for all your application programs to use. The correct printer is selected usually in one of the application's **File** menu options.

Managing Print Jobs

If you want to find out what exactly is happening while a document or documents are being sent to your printer, double-click the printer icon, to open its window.

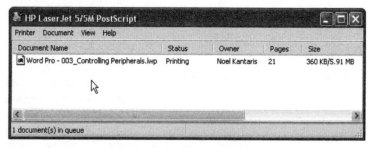

Fig. 3.7 The Print Queue Window.

As shown in Fig. 3.7, this displays detailed information about the contents of any work actually being printed, or of print jobs that are waiting in the queue. This includes the name of the document, its status and 'owner', when it was added to the print queue, the printing progress and when printing was started.

You can control the printing operation from the **Printer** and **Document** menu options of the Print Queue window, from the object menu, or from the **Printer Tasks** list. Selecting **Printer, Pause Printing** will stop the operation until you make the same selection again; it is a toggle menu option. The **Cancel All Documents** option will remove all, or selected, print jobs from the print queue.

Using Fonts

Fonts

Double-clicking the **Fonts** icon in the **Control Panel**, shown here, displays the screen in Fig. 3.8 shown below.

Fig. 3.8 The Fonts Window.

Windows XP uses a Font Manager program to control the installed fonts on your system. You can use the Font Manager to install new fonts, view examples of existing fonts, or delete fonts.

To control what you see on the Fonts window, click **View** to display the drop-down menu, shown in Fig. 3.9 below.

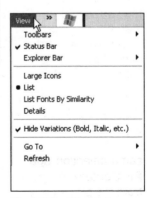

Fig. 3.9 The View Sub-menu.

In this menu, we have chosen the three options; **Status Bar**, **List**, and **Hide Variations**.

To see an example of one of the listed fonts, double-click its icon in the Fonts window to display a screen similar to the one shown in Fig. 3.10 on the next page.

Below we show the Symbol (OpenType) font in three different sizes.

Fig. 3.10 Font Size Sample Window for a Selected Font.

The Symbol font, as you can see, contains an abundance of Greek letters, while the Webdings and Wingdings Fonts contain special graphic objects.

Installing New Fonts

New fonts can be installed by selecting the **File, Install New**  **Font** menu command in the Fonts window, as shown in Fig. 3.11. This opens the Add Fonts dialogue box in which you have to specify the disc, folder and file in which the font you want to install resides.

Unwanted fonts can be removed by first highlighting them in the Fonts window, then using the **File, Delete** command. A warning box is displayed.

Fig. 3.11 Installing New Fonts.

Installing a Fax Printer

Windows XP includes its own Fax printer driver. To install it click the Install a local fax printer option in the Printer Tasks box as shown in Fig. 3.12 below.

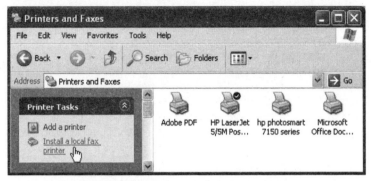

Fig. 3.12 The Printers and Faxes Dialogue box.

This starts the **Install Fax Wizard** which might ask you to insert the Windows XP distribution CD in the CD-ROM drive so that required files can be copied. Once that is done and you supply the information you want to be included in your faxes, a Fax printer is installed in your Printers and Faxes folder, as shown in Fig. 3.13 below.

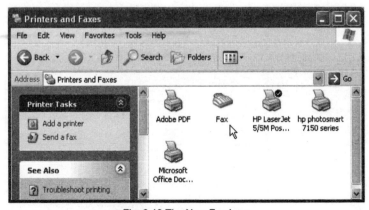

Fig. 3.13 The New Fax Icon.

The Fax Utility

You can use the Fax utility to fax a text document or graphic image as easily as clicking the **Print** icon on an open document in a Windows-based program. Fax supports scanned graphic images and will automatically convert graphics to the appropriate file format before you send them.

To send and receive faxes all you need is a fax device, such as a fax modem - it must support fax capabilities, not just data standards. As we saw in the previous section, installing a fax printer driver is easy. You will have to go through the described procedure as Windows XP does not install the fax printer driver during Windows Setup. Once this is done, you can send faxes from a local fax device attached to your computer, or with a remote fax device connected to fax resources located on a network.

If you have a fax device installed, click *start*, then select **All Programs, Accessories, Communications, Fax** to display the available command options shown in Fig. 3.14.

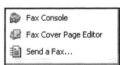

Fig. 3.14 The Fax Menu Options.

Below we give a brief explanation of each fax command option.

The Fax Console: Displays incoming and outgoing faxes and allows you to view and manage your faxes. Clicking this option displays the screen shown in Fig. 3.15.

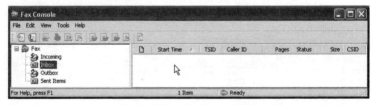

Fig. 3.15 The Fax Console Screen.

The **File** menu options allow you to send a fax (it starts the **Send Fax Wizard** asking you for the recipient's name and other details - you can use the information held in your Address Book, and specify multiple recipients for the one fax), receive a fax now, view, print, save and mail a fax. While a fax is being sent, you can pause or resume its transmission, restart or delete it. You can also import sent or received faxes into the Fax Console.

The **Edit** menu options allow you to select faxes in various ways for further operations.

The **View** menu options allow you to configure what you see and how you see it on the Fax Console.

The **Tools** menu options allow you to enter sender information, create, open, copy or delete personal cover pages, display the fax printer's status, start the **Fax Configuration Wizard**, or display the fax properties and monitor screens.

The Fax Cover Page Editor: Creates and edits cover pages used when sending faxes. The editor allows you to design a template (it also includes drawing facilities), to be used each time you send a fax, as shown in Fig. 3.16 below.

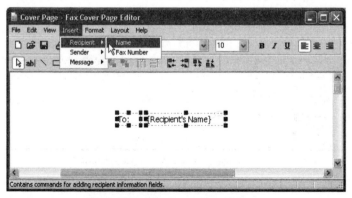

Fig. 3.16 The Fax Cover Page Editor.

As demonstrated previously, you must use the **Insert** menu command to insert what you would like to appear on your fax template, such as recipient's name and fax number, sender's name, fax number, company, address and other details - the field **Note** is where you type the body of your fax. Inserted options can be moved to the desired position on the plate (use the **Ctrl** key to group together fields you want to move together) and formatted accordingly. A simple example is given in Fig. 3.17 below.

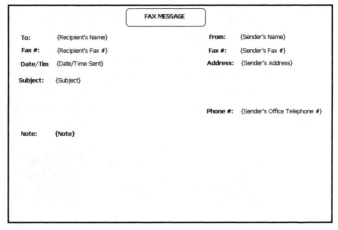

Fig. 3.17 The Designed Cover Page.

The designed template (we hope yours is more imaginative than ours) is saved in the **My Documents\Personal Coverpages** folder with the **.cov** extension.

Send a Fax: Sends a fax that consists only of a cover page. Clicking this menu option starts the **Send Fax Wizard**. This facility should only be used for short messages. If you want to fax a document you should use your word processor and print the document to the Fax printer.

Receiving a Fax

If your computer is switched on and is attached to a fax device, such as a fax modem, a fax sent to you is intercepted by Windows XP which displays the Fax Monitor box shown in Fig. 3.18 below.

Fig. 3.18 The Fax Monitor.

Once the transmission is complete, a warning message appears on the right of the Taskbar, as shown in Fig. 3.19.

Fig. 3.19 The Fax Warning Message.

Clicking the **Fax received** icon on the Taskbar opens the Fax Console, shown in Fig. 3.20 and displays the contents of its **Inbox**.

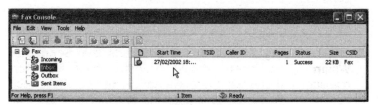

Fig. 3.20 The Fax Console Screen.

Double-clicking an **Inbox** entry, opens the selected Fax in its own window.

The Keyboard

Double-clicking the **Keyboard** icon in the **Control Panel**, shown here, displays the Keyboard Properties dialogue box with its Speed tab selected, as shown in Fig. 3.21.

Fig. 3.21 The Speed Keyboard Properties.

You can use this dialogue box to adjust the amount of time that passes before a character begins to repeat, and the speed at which a character repeats, when you hold down a key, and also adjust the speed at which the insertion pointer blinks. All these adjustments can be carried out by dragging the appropriate slider.

Clicking the Hardware tab, opens the screen shown in Fig. 3.22. Under **Devices**, the name of the keyboard is listed, and under that the name of its manufacturer. If the device is not working properly, click the **Troubleshoot** button.

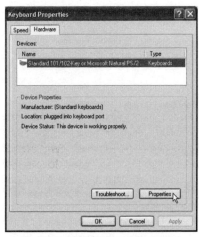

Fig. 3.22 The Hardware Keyboard Properties.

Clicking the **Properties** dialogue box, opens a two-tab dialogue box (not shown here), in which you can either use the troubleshoot facility again, or get information about the device driver and update it if necessary.

The Mouse

To adjust or troubleshoot your mouse, click the **Mouse** button,

Mouse

shown here, in the **Control Panel**, to open the multi-tab Mouse Properties dialogue box shown in Fig. 3.23 below.

Use the Buttons tab screen to switch primary and secondary buttons, depending on whether you are right- or left-handed, adjust the amount of time between clicks when you double-click the primary mouse button, or lock the primary button after a single click, so that you can select or drag items without having to continuously hold down the mouse button. Click again to release ClickLock. To change the time interval before ClickLock takes effect, click the **Settings** button.

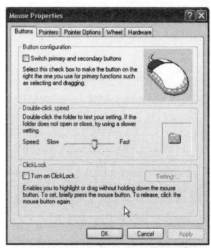

Fig. 3.23 The Mouse Properties Screen.

Mouse Pointer Options

Use the Pointers tab screen to see the default set of pointers used by the system to indicate what action is being carried out at any given moment. You can even build your own set of pointers by using the **Browse** button on the sheet to display and choose from the alternative pointers held in the **Cursors** folder.

Use the Pointer Options tab screen shown in Fig. 3.24 on the next page, to make it more convenient for you to work with the mouse.

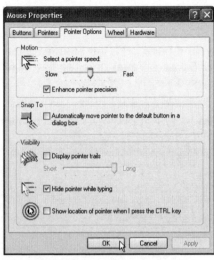

Fig. 3.24 The Mouse Pointer Options Screen.

For example, you can adjust the distance that the pointer moves with respect to the distance covered by the mouse; you can automatically make the pointer snap to the default button in a dialogue box; you can add a trail to the mouse pointer to make it more visible; or you can show the location of the mouse pointer when you press the **Ctrl** key.

If you are using a laptop computer, you will most likely be using its touch pad. In that case, clicking the **Mouse** button on the **Control Panel**, displays the screen in Fig. 3.25 in place of the screen shown in Fig. 3.23.

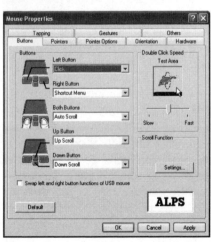

Fig. 3.25 The Mouse Properties Screen.

Most of the options on this dialogue box are self-explanatory and similar to those shown in Fig. 3.23 as already discussed. In this particular Mouse Properties dialogue box, there is even a test area for you to practice double-clicking which displays the animated imagery pointed to in Fig. 3.25.

Phone and Modem Options

Double-clicking the **Phone and Modem Options** icon in the **Control Panel**, shown here, displays the three-tab screen shown in Fig. 3.26 below.

Fig. 3.26 The Phone and Modem Options Screen.

Use these tabbed sheets to add new dialling locations to your computer, or edit existing dialling locations; install a new modem or display and change information about a selected modem; display or configure installed telephony providers on your computer, add to the list, or remove from the list.

Before using your modem, check to ensure it is configured correctly. To do this, click the Modems tab (Fig. 3.26), then in the displayed dialogue box, shown in Fig. 3.27 on the next page, click the **Properties** button, which opens the Properties dialogue box for the installed modem.

Next, select the Diagnostics tab and click the **Query Modem** button, as shown in Fig. 3.28 below in which we show the action to be taken and the result of this action.

If under 'Response' it displays the word 'success' your modem is working fine.

Fig. 3.27 The Modems Tab Screen of the Phone and Modem Options Screen.

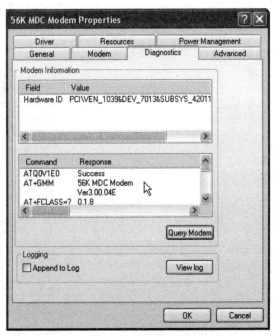

Fig. 3.28 Performing a Diagnostic Test on your Modem.

Scanners and Cameras

Double-clicking the **Scanners and Cameras** icon in the **Control Panel**, shown here, opens the Scanners and Cameras folder shown in Fig. 3.29. Plug and Play Scanners and digital Cameras are detected by Windows XP when they are connected to your PC.

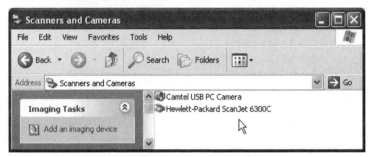

Fig. 3.29 The Scanners and Cameras Folder.

Getting Pictures from a Scanner

After installation, you can start the **Scanner Wizard** by right-clicking the scanner entry in the **Scanners and Cameras**

Fig. 3.30 The Scanner Shortcut Menu.

folder to display a shortcut menu, then click the appropriate option for that device. In Fig. 3.30 we show the shortcut menu for our scanner.

If your scanner is not Plug and Play, follow the instructions that came with that device. It is possible, however, that you might need to get the latest driver for your device which is compatible with Windows XP.

To begin the scanning process, place the picture you want to scan on your scanner's glass plate, then select the **Get picture using Scanner Wizard** option from the shortcut menu in Fig. 3.30. This starts the Wizard and opens the dialogue box shown in Fig. 3.31 on the next page.

As you can see, in this instance we have three scanning choices; colour, grey-scale, or black and white.

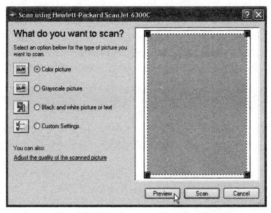

Fig. 3.31 The Scanner Dialogue Box.

Clicking the **Preview** button will activate the scanner and a preview of the object will appear on the right side of the Scanner dialogue box, as shown in Fig. 3.32.

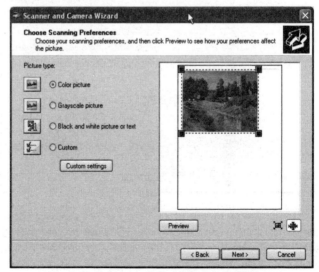

Fig. 3.32 Cropping a Scanned Picture in Preview.

In the picture preview in Fig. 3.32 on the previous page, we also show how you can crop the size of the scanned image to the required size of the picture by dragging the square handles to the correct position.

Clicking the **Next** button displays additional Wizard screens asking you to specify the name of the picture and where you would like its file to be saved. As usual, you move through successive Wizard screens by clicking the **Next** button, until the penultimate screen where you are asked whether you would like to 'Publish the picture to a Web site', 'order prints from a photo printing Web site', or do 'Nothing' because you have finished. Selecting the last option, saves your picture in the specified folder, opens the folder and highlights its filename.

Double-clicking the selected filename, displays your picture in the **Windows Picture and Fax Viewer**, as shown in Fig. 3.33 - it looks better in colour!

Fig. 3.33 A Scanned Picture in the Windows Picture and Fax Viewer.

Clicking the button pointed to at the bottom of the picture, closes the Picture and Fax Viewer and opens the displayed picture in the Microsoft Photo Editor where you can use your editing skills to completely transform it.

Getting Pictures from a Camera

If you have a digital camera, Windows usually detects it the moment you plug it in and loads the appropriate driver for it. Also, digital cameras are sold with their own software on CD, on which you will find not only the correct driver for your camera, but also other application programs that make it easy to download pictures to your computer.

One of our cameras displays the three screens shown in Fig. 3.34, in succession, when it is connected to the PC and is switched on. It automatically finds the pictures in the camera, copies them to the PC, and ends the process.

Fig. 3.34 Image Transfer Software.

The pictures in our camera are downloaded to the folder we specified in the **Settings** menu option of the software. To see these pictures, navigate to the appropriate folder and use the **View**, **Filmstrip** menu command.

In your case the downloading procedure will most likely be different, unless you happen to have the same camera supported by the same software as ours, but we expect it will be just as easy.

4

Software Upkeep

In this chapter we will examine how you can install or remove programs and Windows components from your computer, how to update Windows in order to keep your operating system fine-tuned, how to use the Backup program to protect your data, and how to schedule tasks to automate certain processes.

Adding New Software to your PC

To add new Windows programs to your computer's hard disc, use the *start*, **Control Panel** command, and click the **Add or Remove Programs** icon, shown here to the left. This examines your hard disc for installed programs and displays its contents in a window similar to the one shown in Fig. 4.1 below.

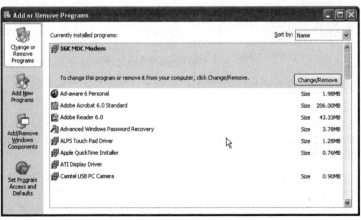

Fig. 4.1 The Add or Remove Programs Screen.

Next, click the **Add New Programs** button on the left pane of the displayed dialogue box, which changes to the one shown in Fig. 4.2.

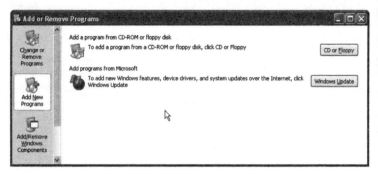

Fig. 4.2 The Add New Programs Screen.

This facility to add programs seems superfluous because installing new Windows programs on your computer's hard disc is made very easy these days. Almost all Windows applications are distributed on one or more CDs the first one of which uses an auto-run program which in turn runs the Setup program.

Furthermore, most applications vendors give you instructions that if the auto-run program does not start the

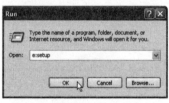

Fig. 4.3 The Run Dialogue Box.

installation process, to click the Windows *start* button, and select the **Run** command which opens the Run dialogue box shown in Fig. 4.3 and type in the **Open** text box the command

    e:\setup

where e: is our CD-ROM drive; yours will probably be different. Clicking the **OK** button, starts the installation process.

In the end, which method you use, if the auto-run facility fails, is up to you.

Adding/Removing Windows Features

The **Add/Remove Windows Components** icon in Fig. 4.1, allows you to install or remove specific Windows components at any time. Clicking this icon, opens the dialogue box shown in Fig. 4.4. Next, highlight the group that you think will contain what you want to add or remove, and click the **Details** button.

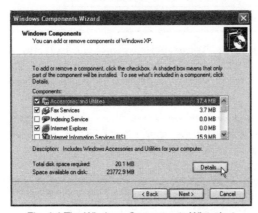

Fig. 4.4 The Windows Components Wizard.

This examines your system and lists the components of the chosen group, as shown in Fig. 4.5. Clicking the box to the left of an item name will install the selected component, while any items with their ticks removed, will be uninstalled.

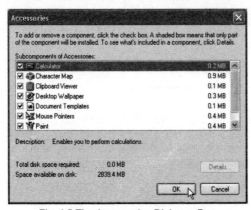

Fig. 4.5 The Accessories Dialogue Box.

You will need to have the original Windows XP CD available, and when you have made the selections you want, keep clicking **OK** to carry out the required changes. It is easy to use up too much hard disc space with Windows XP features, so keep your eye on the **Total disk space required** entry.

Change or Remove Programs

The **Change or Remove Programs** icon on the left pane of the Add or Remove Programs dialogue box (Fig. 4.6) only works for programs on your system that were specially written for Windows and are listed in the displayed window.

To change or remove a listed application, highlight it, then click the **Change/Remove** buttons to the right of the highlighted area as shown in Fig. 4.6 below.

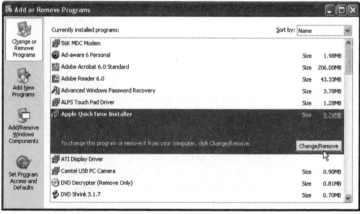

Fig. 4.6 The Add or Remove Programs Screen.

A warning box will be displayed before a program is removed, giving you the chance to change your mind. If you confirm your decision to remove the highlighted program, a Wizard will start and the program will be uninstalled.

Using this option removes all traces of the selected program from your hard disc.

Reinstalling a Program

If you attempt to reinstall an already installed program, by either using the auto-run facility or any of the other two methods discussed earlier, you will be given the chance to either install additional features to the program, reinstall it completely, or remove it from your hard disc. Obviously, not all programs give you the same facilities. For example, in Fig. 4.7, we show the first screen that displays if you attempt to reinstall the Microsoft Works 2004 suite of programs.

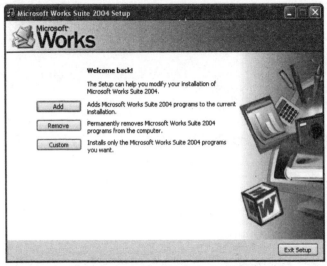

Fig. 4.7 The Microsoft Works Welcome Screen.

As you can see, the program has detected a current installation and displays the message **Welcome back!** The facilities offered here are **Add**, **Remove**, or **Custom**.

The Windows Update Utility

An essential part of keeping your Windows system healthy and up-to-date is the Update program. Microsoft provides fixes and updates to Windows XP and its many other components on their Web site. The Update program behaves differently for pre- or post-Service Pack 2 installation.

Update Utility Prior to Service Pack 2

To run the Windows Update Utility, click *start*, **All Programs** and select the **Windows Update** option on the cascade menu.

When you first invoke the Update program you are asked to connect to the Internet, if you are using a Dial-up Connection. Once connection is established, the screen in Fig. 4.8 is displayed.

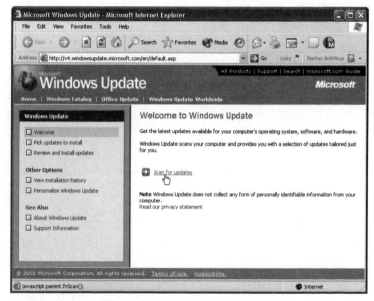

Fig. 4.8 The Windows Update Screen.

Clicking the **Scan for updates** link, starts the process by first looking into your computer's configuration to see what your system might need, before displaying the updates relevant to your system. In our case the screen in Fig. 4.9 on the next page was displayed. In your case the contents of this screen will most certainly be different from ours. It all depends on when you updated your system last time, and what you selected to download from the site at the time.

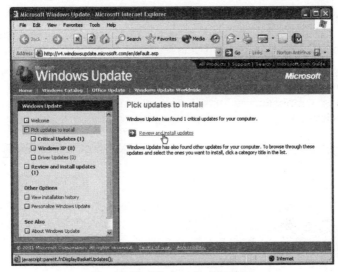

Fig. 4.9 The Windows Updates List.

Using the above screen you can **Review and install updates** you select from the displayed list, as shown in Fig. 4.10 below.

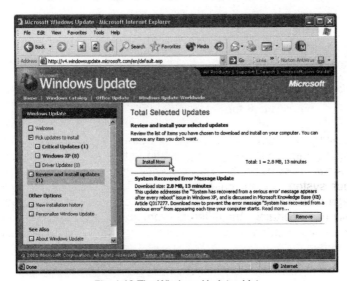

Fig. 4.10 The Windows Updates List.

Update Utility with Service Pack 2

If you have installed Service Pack 2, invoking Windows Update, displays the screen in Fig. 4.11

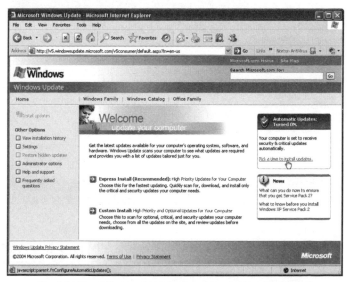

Fig. 4.11 The Windows Update Screen under Service Pack 2.

Note that in this case, Automatic Updates is turned ON. This has been configured either by clicking the **Automatic Updates** icon in **Control Panel**, shown here, or by clicking the link pointed to in Fig. 4.11 above. Either of these actions opens the dialogue box in Fig. 4.12 in which you can set the day and time for the Automatic Updates.

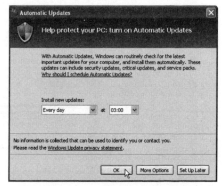

Fig. 4.12 The Automatic Updates Box.

The Administrative Tools

Double-clicking the **Administrative Tools** icon in the **Control Panel**, opens the folder, shown in Fig. 4.13, which provides shortcuts to certain Management tools and services.

Fig. 4.13 The Administrative Tools Folder.

For example, Component Services provides access to Management Services which host administrative tools that you can use to administer networks, PCs, services, and other system components; while Computer Management provides access to a collection of administrative tools that you can use to manage a single local or remote PC.

Clicking the System Monitor shortcut displays a colourful screen which shows the detailed monitoring of the operating system resources, as shown in Fig. 4.14.

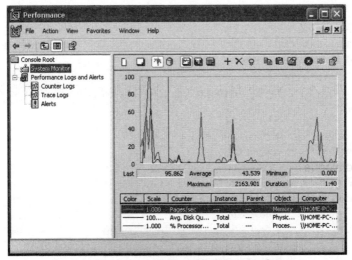

Fig. 4.14 The System Performance Monitoring Screen.

The Backup Utility

Windows XP comes with a Backup Utility which is installed by default in the Professional Edition, but has to be installed manually in the Home Edition. The Backup utility is included on the Windows XP Home Edition CD-ROM in the ValueAdd folder, but it does not support the **Automated System Recovery Wizard**.

To manually install Backup:

*   Double-click the NTBackup.msi file in the

    e:\ValueAdd\msft\NTBackup

    location on the Windows XP Home Edition CD, where e: is our CD-ROM drive (yours might be different).

*   Follow the instructions of the Wizard and when installation is complete, click **Finish**.

The Backup utility is accessible via the *start*, **All Programs**, **Accessories**, **System Tools** cascade menu. It is a utility that can be used to back up both system set-up and data files from the hard disc to another, removable storage medium, on a regular basis.

Hard discs can 'crash' (but not as often now as they used to) and your computer could be stolen, or lost in a fire or flood. Any of these events would cause a serious data loss, particularly to businesses, unless you had backed it all up, and stored it somewhere safely, preferably away from the vicinity of your PC.

Making a Backup

We will step through the procedure of backing up, and then restoring, a selection of files. You should then be happy to carry on by yourself. Using the *start*, **All Programs**, **Accessories**, **System Tools**, cascade menu command and clicking the **Backup** icon, shown here, starts the **Backup or Restore Wizard**, as shown in Fig. 4.15 on the next page.

Fig. 4.15 The Windows XP Professional Backup Welcome Screen.

Note the **Advanced Mode** link pointed to in Fig. 4.15 above. Clicking on this link allows you to schedule backups. We will look at this facility later.

The backup procedure can be carried out on a tape, a floppy disc, or a removable disc. Clicking the **Next** button displays the second Wizard screen where we chose to **Back up files and settings,** and in the third Wizard screen we selected the **Let me choose what to back up** option. In the fourth Wizard screen, shown in Fig. 4.16 on the next page, we selected the **My Documents** folder by clicking the + sign to open its structure in the left-hand pane, then double-clicking the **My Pictures** folder to check it.

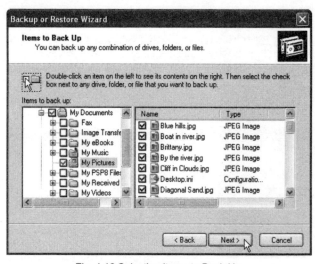

Fig. 4.16 Selecting items to Back Up.

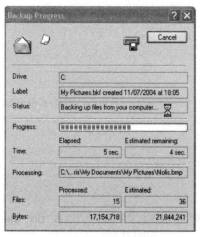

Fig. 4.17 Backing Up Process.

To select, or deselect, individual files, tick in their boxes in the right-hand pane, as shown above, and press the **Next** button. The **Backup Wizard** asks you to select what and where to back up, give a name to your back-up file that means something to you in the future, gives you a summary of what is intended, and lets you start the process. The window shown in Fig. 4.17, keeps you informed during the backing up process.

Backup Types

By default, during our demonstration, we have created a 'Normal' backup of the selected files. To see what other types of backup exist, first return to the opening screen of the **Backup or Restore Wizard**, then click the **Advanced Mode** link to display the screen in Fig. 4.18.

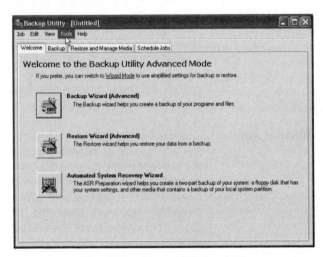

Fig. 4.18 The Advanced Backup Utility.

Next, use the **Tools, Options** command to open the Options dialogue box shown in Fig. 4.19.

The Backup utility supports five methods of backing up data on your computer or network. These are listed on the next page.

Fig. 4.19 Selecting the Backup Type.

Normal Backup
Copies all selected files and marks them as having been backed up. With normal backups, you need only the most recent copy of the backup file or tape to restore all of the files. A normal backup is usually performed the first time you create a backup set.

Copy Backup
Copies all selected files but does not mark them as having been backed up. Copying is useful if you want to back up files between normal and incremental backups because it does not affect these other backup operations.

Differential Backup
Copies files created or changed since the last normal or incremental backup. It does not mark files as having been backed up. If you are performing a combination of normal and differential backups, restoring files and folders requires that you have the last normal as well as the last differential backup.

Incremental Backup
Backs up only those files created or changed since the last normal or incremental backup. It marks files as having been backed up. If you use a combination of normal and incremental backups, you will need to have the last normal backup set as well as all incremental backup sets in order to restore your data.

Daily Backup
Copies all selected files that have been modified on the day the daily backup is performed. The backed-up files are not marked as having been backed up.

If the data files you are backing up are not very large in size, then using a normal backup is the easiest method. The backup set is stored on one disc or tape and restoring data from it is very easy.

If the amount of your storage space is limited, then back up your data using a combination of normal and incremental backups; it is the quickest method. However, recovering files can be time-consuming and difficult because the backup set can be stored on several discs or tapes.

Finally, backing up your data using a combination of normal and differential backups is more time-consuming, especially if your data changes frequently, but it is easier to restore because the backup set is usually stored on only a few discs or tapes.

Restoring your Files

To restore files that have been previously backed up, place the first disc of the set in the disc drive, activate the **Backup or Restore Wizard** and on the second Wizard screen click the Restore radio button followed by **Next**. Again, click the + sign to open the file structure in the left-hand pane of the Restore window, as shown in Fig. 4.20. In this way you can choose to restore individual components of the backup set.

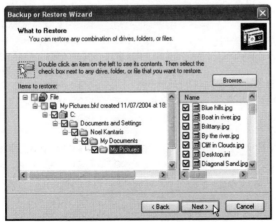

Fig. 4.20 Selecting the Backup Set to Restore.

Pressing the **Next** button, displays a Summary screen of the restore procedure. Clicking the **Advanced** button on this Summary screen, gives you a choice on where to restore the selected items, then what to do when restoring files that already exist, as shown in Fig. 4.21.

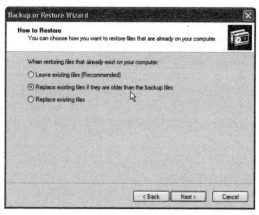

Fig. 4.21 Selecting How to Restore.

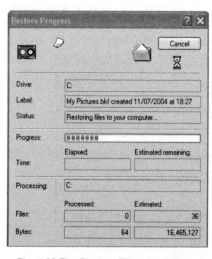

Fig. 4.22 The Restore Progress Screen.

A good choice would be to select the option to 'Replace the file on disk only if it is older than the backup copy'. After making an appropriate selection on file replacement and file security, pressing the **Finish** button causes the Wizard to start the restore process, as shown in Fig. 4.22.

Hopefully you should by now be completely sold on the Backup utility.

Scheduled Tasks

Using the *start*, **All Programs**, **Accessories**, **System Tools**,

cascade menu command and clicking the **Schedule Tasks** icon, shown here, displays the screen shown in Fig. 4.23 below.

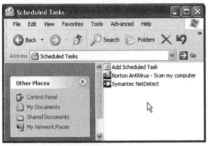

Fig. 4.23 The Scheduled Tasks Window.

The Scheduled Tasks window allows you to carry out several Windows XP house-keeping tasks, such as data backup, or disc cleanup, at times convenient to you.

If you are running other programs, such as Norton AntiVirus in our case, an entry for that program also appears in the Scheduled window (Fig. 4.23).

To add a scheduled Windows XP task, double-click the **Add Scheduled Task** icon to start the Wizard. Clicking **Next** on the first Wizard screen displays the second Wizard screen, shown in Fig. 4.24 below:

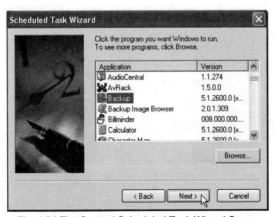

Fig. 4.24 The Second Scheduled Task Wizard Screen.

On this screen (Fig. 4.24), select the task to be scheduled then click the **Next** button to display:

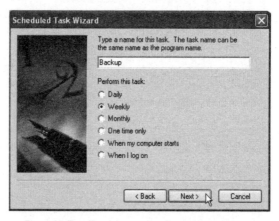

Fig. 4.25 The Third Scheduled Task Wizard Screen.

On this screen (Fig. 4.25) you are asked to specify the frequency at which you would like the selected task to be performed (we selected weekly in our example). Having done so, press the **Next** button to display the fourth Wizard screen, shown in Fig. 4.26, where you are asked to specify when you want the selected task to be carried out.

Fig. 4.26 The Fourth Scheduled Task Wizard Screen.

Obviously, your computer must be switched on at the specified day and time. Having done so, press the **Next** button to display the fifth Wizard screen shown in Fig. 4.27 below.

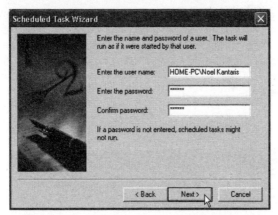

Fig. 4.27 The Fifth Scheduled Task Wizard Screen.

As you can see on the above Wizard screen, you can enter the name of a user and their password. The task is then run as if it were started by the specified user. Clicking **Next**, displays an additional screen (in the case of Backup), as shown in Fig. 4.28.

Fig. 4.28 The Sixth Scheduled Backup Wizard Screen.

After providing additional information, click the **OK** button to display the final Wizard screen and clicking the **Finish** button, performs the selected task at its chosen time.

It is a good idea to perform such tasks regularly, but make sure that your computer is switched on at the selected times, and you are not inconvenienced by your time selection. It is, of course, assumed that your PC's clock is showing the same time as your watch, otherwise you might get some unexpected surprises!

The newly created scheduled task now appears in the Scheduled Tasks window, as shown in Fig. 4.29 below.

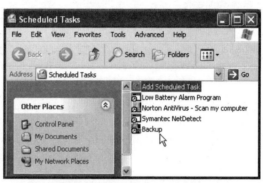

Fig. 4.29 The Additional Entry in the Scheduled Tasks Window.

To edit a scheduled task, double-click its entry in the above window, which opens the three-tab dialogue box of Fig. 4.27, shown on the previous page, in which you can make changes to the selected 'Task', its 'Schedule', and its 'Settings'.

5

Hardware Upkeep

Adding Hardware to your System

Windows XP automates the process of adding hardware to your system by including a set of software standards for controlling suitably designed hardware devices.

Plug-and-Play: Windows supports what are known as Plug-and-Play compatible devices. So, when you buy new hardware, make sure that it is Plug-and-Play compatible. Adding such hardware devices to your system is extremely easy, as Windows takes charge and automatically controls all its settings so that it fits in with the rest of the system.

Add New Hardware Wizard: If your new hardware is not Plug-and-Play compatible all is not lost, as there is a very powerful Wizard to help you with their installation. Fit the new hardware before you run the Wizard, as it is just possible that Windows will recognise the change and be able to carry out the configuration by itself.

If the new hardware is not recognised, start the Wizard by double-clicking the **Add New Hardware** icon in the **Control**

Panel, shown here, and follow the instructions. The Wizard searches your system for anything new, which takes a few seconds to complete. Then, if the new hardware is not recognised, a list of the installed hardware is displayed and you are asked to specify the type of new hardware.

If your new hardware has come with a CD and Windows asks you, insert it in the CD-ROM drive, as Windows might need hardware drivers which are usually supplied by the hardware manufacturer.

Disk Cleanup

The first thing that the **Disk Cleanup** utility does after activation, whether from the **Scheduled Tasks** or by clicking its icon, shown here, in the *start*, **All Programs**, **Accessories**, **System Tools** menu, is to ask you to select the drive you want to clean up, as shown in Fig. 5.1. It then scans the specified drive, and then lists temporary files, Internet cache files, and unnecessary program files that you can safely delete, as shown in Fig. 5.2 below.

Fig. 5.1 Selecting a Drive.

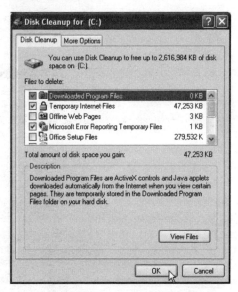

Fig. 5.2 Files Found by Cleanup.

As you can see, in our case, we could free 47,253 KB of disc space by simply deleting the Temporary Internet Files (Web pages stored on your hard disc for quick viewing). The More Options tab allows you to remove Windows components and installed programs that you do not use any more.

De-fragmenting your Hard Discs

The **Disk Defragmenter** can also be scheduled to optimise a
 hard disc by rearranging the data on it to eliminate
unused spaces, which speeds up access to the disc by
Windows operations. You can also activate this utility
by clicking its icon, shown here, in the *start*, **All Programs**,
Accessories, **System Tools** menu.

You don't need to exit a running application before starting
the **Disk Defragmenter**. Once activated, choose which drive to
de-fragment and you can do so in the background while
working by minimising the utility onto the Task bar. On the
other hand, you can watch the process of the operation.

For example, having selected a drive and clicked the
Analyze button, you will be told whether de-fragmentation is
needed or not. Next, clicking the **Defragment** button, starts the
process which is shown in Fig. 5.3 below.

Fig. 5.3 De-fragmentation in Progress.

On your screen you can see which files are fragmented (shown
in red) and which files are not fragmented (shown in blue),
while free space is shown in white. For large drives this
process can take a long time, so make time for it!

Scanning a Hard Disc for Errors

Windows XP incorporates a utility that can check the integrity of your hard disc, and if it finds any errors, it can attempt to repair them. To start this utility, click **My Computer** then in the displayed screen right-click the drive you want to check, select **Properties** from the drop-down menu and click the Tools tab to display the screen in Fig. 5.4.

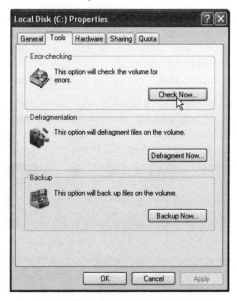

Fig. 5.4 The Disk Properties Screen.

As you can see, you have three choices; **Check Now** for disc errors, **Defragment Now**, or **Backup Now**. The last option is not available in the Windows XP Home edition.

Before you can start scanning your selected drive for errors, all running programs and applications on that drive must be closed. If you start this utility while a program on that drive is running, you will be informed of the fact in a warning box. If your disc or disc partition is formatted as NTFS (see next section), Windows automatically logs all file transactions, replaces bad clusters, and stores copies of key information for all files on the NTFS disc or disc partition.

Drive Conversion to NTFS

If you did not choose to convert your Windows XP drive from the FAT file system to the NTFS file system during installation, you can do so at any time. However, before doing so, you must consider the various advantages and disadvantages associated with such a conversion.

- Do not convert your Windows XP drive to the NTFS file system if you intend to retain your Windows 95/98/Me installation, and you want to exchange document files between the two systems (in both directions).

- Convert to NTFS if you want to get better file security, including the Encrypting File System (EFS) which protects data on your hard drive by encrypting each file with a randomly generated key.

- Convert to NTFS if you want better disc compression and better support for large hard discs.

- Convert to NTFS if you have a large hard drive and don't want its performance to degrade as it does with the FAT or FAT32 system.

Finally, from an NTFS partition you can browse, read and write to files on the FAT or FAT32 partitions, but Windows 95/98/Me cannot detect the NTFS partition, so it cannot interfere with its settings. However, the conversion to NTFS is one-way, therefore, you will not be able to convert back to FAT or FAT32.

To convert your Windows XP FAT or FAT32 drive to NTFS, click on **Start** then select **All Programs, Accessories, Command Prompt** option, then type the following commands in two lines, pressing the **Enter** key at the end of each line, as shown in Fig. 5.5 below.

cd\
Convert C:/fs:ntfs

Fig. 5.5 Command Prompt.

System Restore

The System Restore sheet of the System Properties screen, allows you to turn off System Restore (not advisable) or change the drive settings or the amount of disc space available to System Restore on a selected drive.

If things go really wrong, System Restore can be used to return your PC to the last date it was working properly. Every time you start to install a new program, Windows XP takes a snapshot of your system prior to starting the new installation. Alternatively, you can force Windows to take a snapshot any time you choose.

To examine the System Restore utility, click the **System Restore** icon, shown here, in the *start*, **All Programs**, **Accessories**, **System Tools** menu. This opens the Welcome to System Restore screen shown in Fig. 5.6.

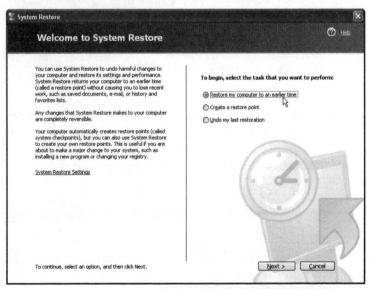

Fig. 5.6 The Welcome to System Restore Screen.

As you can see, you can select to Restore your computer to an earlier time, or create a Restore point.

As an example, we chose the **Restore my computer to an earlier time** option, then clicked the **Next** button. This displays a further screen, as shown in Fig. 5.7 below.

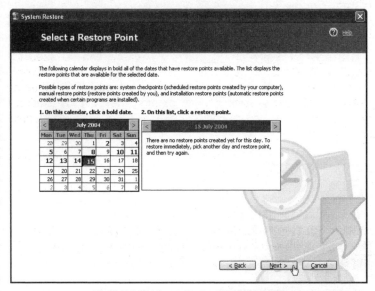

Fig. 5.7 Selecting a System Restore Point.

The dates shown in bold in the calendar are Restore points created by Windows XP. The three possible types of Restore points are:

- System Restore points created by your computer

- Manual Restore points created by you

- Restore points automatically created prior to installing certain programs.

If you select to create a Manual Restore point, Windows XP asks you to give a description of this Restore point so that you can identify it easily at a later stage, as shown in Fig. 5.8 on the next page.

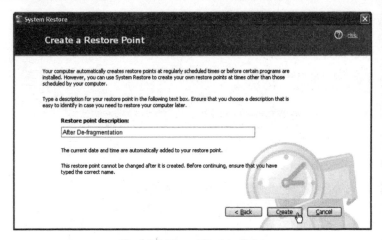

Fig. 5.8 A Manual Restore Point.

Having typed in a **Restore point description**, click the **Create** button to create it. This will show today's date with the description attached to it so that you can easily identify it later, as shown in Fig. 5.9.

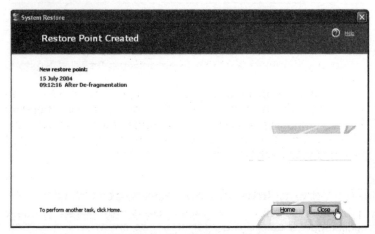

Fig. 5.9 The Created Restore Point.

The importance of Creating Restore points cannot be stressed enough (see Chapter 11).

System Properties

Clicking the **System** icon, shown here, in the **Control Panel**, displays the System Properties dialogue box shown in Fig. 5.10 below.

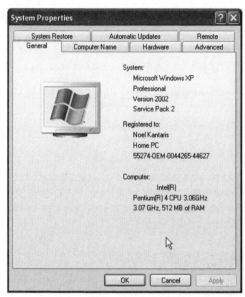

Fig. 5.10 The General Tab-sheet of the System Properties Screen.

The System Properties multi-tab dialogue box provides you with basic information about your computer, its operating software, and its peripheral drivers. Some, but by no means all, of this information you can change. Below we give a short description of each tab sheet.

The General Information Tab-sheet

The General sheet of the System Properties screen, displays which version of Windows is installed on your PC, as shown in Fig. 5.10 above. It also specifies registration information for your copy of Windows, and specifies the type of processor and the total physical memory of your PC.

Computer Name

The Computer Name sheet of the System Properties screen, provides a space for you to type a descriptive name for your PC. It also identifies the group to which it belongs and provides you with the means to change it.

Fig. 5.11 The Computer Name Tab-sheet of the System Properties Screen.

The Hardware Tab-sheet

The Hardware sheet of the System Properties screen, allows you to use the **Hardware Wizard** to detect new hardware and change device properties. You can also use the Device Manager to change the properties and resource settings of hardware devices, and to copy or rename a hardware profile.

Clicking the **Device Manager** button on the Hardware tab-sheet, displays the screen shown in Fig. 5.12 on the next page.

On this screen, all the devices connected to your computer are shown. Clicking the ⊞ box appearing in front of a device, displays additional information about that particular device. All the opened devices here are shown as working OK - there are no marks of any kind against their name.

If a device attached to your computer does not work, check here to see if a large yellow question mark displays against the particular device. If it does, then this indicates that the device does not work properly. One solution might be that you need to upgrade the device's driver - but not necessarily the only reason.

Fig. 5.12 Devices Connected to your Computer.

The Advanced Tab-sheet

The Advanced sheet of the System Properties screen, allows you to change settings for program resources, visual effects, and memory usage. You can also change the default operating system that starts when you turn on your computer.

Note: Before you change anything, be it a device driver or any of the settings that you can reach from the Device Manager, do read carefully the relevant help pages provided by Microsoft, by clicking the **Help** icon on the Device Manager's toolbar pointed to in Fig. 5.12 above. One screen of this extensive Help facility with appropriate warning, is shown in Fig. 5.13 on the next page.

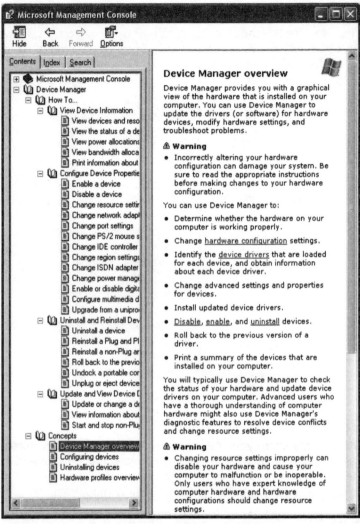

Fig. 5.13 The Device Manager Help Screen.

As you can see, there is a lot of help here, as well as a lot of 'Warnings'. So, before you do anything, spend some time reading as much as necessary!

The Remote Tab-sheet

The Remote tab-sheet of the System Properties screen, shown in Fig. 5.14, allows you to activate remote assistance which allows a friend in another location to connect to your computer from another computer running a compatible operating system.

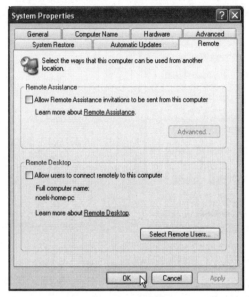

Fig. 5.14 The Remote Tab-sheet of the System Properties Screen.

After connection, your friend can view your computer screen and, with your permission, assist you to correct a problem by taking control of your PC.

Finally, you could use the Automatic Updates tab-sheet to keep your computer up to date, as we discussed in Chapter 4, page 68.

The Game Controllers

Clicking the **Game Controllers** icon in **Control Panel**, shown here, opens the dialogue box in Fig. 5.15. Normally, if you had any game controllers installed on your computer they will be listed here. If you wanted to test, configure,

or re-calibrate a controller you would select it from the list and click the **Properties** button.

The Games Folder

We will not spend long on this topic. In Windows XP the games folder can be reached from the *start*, **All Programs** cascade menu.

Fig. 5.16 The Games Folder.

Fig. 5.15 The Game Controllers Screen.

The **Games** folder contains 11 games, as shown in Fig. 5.16. Of these, five games require you to connect to the Internet to find opponents of different skill levels, while the other six can be played without additional expense. Classic Hearts can be played over a network against real opponents or against opponents supplied by the computer. FreeCell is a patience based game, while Classic Solitaire, Minesweeper, Spider Solitaire are designed to help with mouse skills. Pinball is a 3D arcade type game with impressive sounds that tests your reactions.

All of these games come with quite good Help sections and we will leave it to you to explore them at your leisure!

6

Internet Connections

In this chapter we will examine how you can connect your PC to the Internet, before discussing how to publish a file or folder to the Web, followed by how to change user accounts settings and passwords.

The Internet Options

Clicking the **Internet Options** icon in the **Control Panel**, shown here, opens the dialogue box in Fig. 6.1 below.

In the General tab sheet, you specify which page to use for your Home page (the one that is displayed when you first open Internet Explorer). You can also **Delete Cookies** (information created and stored on your hard disc by Web sites you visited).

Fig. 6.1 The Internet Properties Dialogue Box.

You can also **Delete Files** which are temporary Internet files holding information on pages you visited before on a Web site. These files allow you to browse quickly through such pages because your Internet browser checks and uses them (if the information in them has not changed) in preference to downloading them from the Internet, which takes much longer.

Fig. 6.2 The Settings Dialogue Box.

Obviously such temporary Internet files can take a lot of hard disc space, but you can control this by clicking the **Settings** button to open the dialogue box shown in Fig. 6.2. In here you can select from several options for checking for newer versions of stored Web pages, and you can limit the amount of hard disc space used by them. Click the **View Files** button to see a list of the temporary files held on your computer.

Going back to the General tab sheet of the Internet Properties dialogue box, you will see options at the bottom of the box dealing with **History**. This is a folder that holds links to pages you have visited, for quick access to recently viewed Web site pages without having to connect to the Internet.

To view history links, click the **History** Toolbar button, shown here to the right, on a Windows XP application such as the **Internet Explorer** or **My Computer** (to do this, use the **View**, **Toolbars**, **Customize** menu command), to open the History panel, shown in Fig. 6.3. You can choose History links from **Today** to several **Weeks Ago**.

Fig. 6.3 The History Panel.

Internet Security

If you want to stop people getting at your data or tracking what you are doing, then Internet security is important to you.

Fig. 6.4 The Internet Security Screen.

Clicking the Security tab of the Internet Properties dialogue box displays the sheet shown in Fig. 6.4. As each item under **Select a Web content zone to specify its security settings** at the top of the screen is selected, its security settings are shown below the selection area. For example, when **Internet** is selected, you are told that 'This zone contains all Web sites you haven't placed in other zones'. To change the settings, click the **Custom Level** button to display the Security Settings dialogue box shown in Fig. 6.5. In this screen you can select settings for various **ActiveX controls**. These are potentially risky actions, with some of the options not providing a **Prompt** setting.

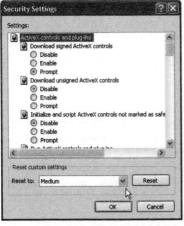

Fig. 6.5 The Security Settings Screen.

None of these options apply to FTP folders, which are folders you upload or download to or from Web sites using the File Transfer Protocol which, however, does not use encryption or other security mechanism to protect your password when you log on to a server. If you want such security, then use Web folders instead.

Internet Privacy

Clicking the Privacy tab of the Internet Properties dialogue box displays the screen in Fig. 6.6. On here you can specify the

Fig. 6.6 The Internet Privacy Screen.

Fig. 6.7 The Advanced Privacy Settings Screen.

security level for the Internet zone. As you move the slide up a notch at a time, you impose higher and higher security, while moving the slide downwards diminishes it. An explanation on what is allowed and what is not, is given next to the slide as you move it to a different level. You can also override cookie handling for individual Web sites by clicking **Edit** and filling in the displayed sheet.

Clicking the **Advanced** button, displays the screen shown in Fig. 6.7, in which you can control cookies. If the override box (pointed to) is not checked, the options under it are greyed out. In that case, the Web site's privacy policy, if it exists, is displayed by **Internet Explorer**, which tells you what kind of information the Web site collects, and how it uses it. Also, Web sites might provide a (P3P) (Platform for Privacy Preferences Policy), in which case **Internet Explorer** might be able to compare your privacy settings to that of the P3P privacy policy, and determine whether or not to allow the Web site to save cookies on your PC. If you check the override box, then you must decide how first-party and third-party cookies should be treated.

Internet Content

Clicking the Content tab of the Internet Properties dialogue box

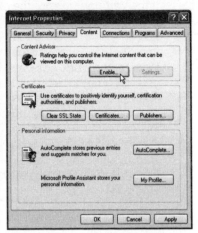

Fig. 6.8 The Internet Content Screen.

Fig. 6.9 The Content Advisor Screen.

displays the screen in Fig. 6.8. The most important option on this screen is the **Content Advisor** which helps you to control the Internet content that can be viewed on your computer. Clicking the **Enable** button displays the screen shown in Fig. 6.9, where you can set ratings on Language, Nudity, Sex, and Violence permitted to be viewed.

You set these ratings by selecting each option and moving the slide to the right a notch at a time, which lowers the level of restriction. What is allowed to be viewed is displayed in the **Description** box as you move the slide. Once you have set ratings to all the listed options, click the **Apply** button followed by **OK**. This displays the Create Supervisor Password dialogue box so that you can protect these ratings.

Other options on the Content tab screen of the Internet Properties dialogue box, allow you to use **Certificates** to identify yourself, change the **AutoComplete** settings, or specify **Personal information** you can share when a Web site requests information from its visitors.

Internet Connection Options

Clicking the Connections tab of the Internet Properties

Fig. 6.10 The Internet Connections Tab-sheet.

dialogue box displays the screen in Fig. 6.10. Under the **Dial-up and Virtual Private Network settings** you will see a list of our Internet connections which are already available on this computer. However, to show you how to make such connections, we will take you through the steps required.

To set up a new Internet connection, click the **Setup** button which starts the **New Connection Wizard** shown in Fig. 6.11.

Fig. 6.11 The New Connection Wizard.

As you can see, this Wizard can be used to connect to the Internet or a private network, or set up a home or small office network. For networking, see Chapter 7.

Below, we will look at, and guide you through, the two main types of Internet connection: Dial-up modem, and Broadband.

Connection Using a Dial-up Modem

To proceed with the Wizard, click the **Next** button, then:

- In the first Wizard screen, select the **Connect to the Internet** option from those available and click **Next**.

- In the second Wizard screen, select the **Set up my connection manually** option and click **Next**.

- In the third Wizard screen, select the **Connect using a dial-up modem** option and click **Next**.

- In the fourth Wizard screen, (Fig. 6.12), type in your ISP's name and click **Next**.

Fig. 6.12 The Fourth New Connection Wizard Screen.

- In the fifth Wizard screen, type in the phone number of your ISP.

- In the sixth Wizard screen, shown in Fig. 6.13, type in the **User Name** and **Password** given to you by your ISP, tick the boxes relevant to you, then click **Next**.

- The final Wizard screen displays a summary of your entries, and click- ing **Finish** creates

Fig. 6.13 The Sixth New Connection Wizard Screen.

the connection and closes down the Wizard.

Now, whenever you activate Internet Explorer of your e-mail program, such as Outlook Express or Microsoft Outlook, the screen shown in Fig. 6.14 is displayed on your screen, ready for you to make the connection to your ISP.

Fig. 6.14 The Dial-up Connection Screen.

Connections Using Broadband

To use broadband, you must first select a Broadband ISP, who might or might not charge you a connection/installation fee, or provide you with a free broadband modem - see next page for choice of available modems, which are dependant on the type of connection required. A quick search on the Internet (try www.google.com) will unveil the most current offers, but before choosing, look at pricing and restrictions associated with particular connections.

Monthly connection fees depend on a choice of connection speeds which can vary from 5 times to 15 times the speed of a dial-up (56 Kbps) modem, the most typical one being 10 times (512 Kbps) for domestic use. Other factors that control pricing can be the availability of e-mail addresses, mail filtering, and Web site hosting. However, keep an eye on restrictions - some providers only allow certain amount of Internet browsing a month, others do not allow you to play games on-line, while others only allow one computer to be connected to the Internet.

Next, you must find out whether your premises are near enough to the exchange and whether broadband is available at that particular exchange. Both of these requirements can be found out quickly and easily by simply selecting the appropriate option on you chosen ISP's Web site, and typing in your postcode.

If all is well, you can now select the type of broadband modem you require. Broadly speaking, there are three types of modems you might want to use as a domestic user. These are:

1. A simple broadband modem which connects to your computer's USB port. This is the type most commonly provided free by ISPs and can only connect a single computer.

2. A broadband modem that provides both a USB and an Ethernet (LAN) connection. This type can use either connection for broadband, or use the LAN port to connect two computers together and the USB port to connect to broadband.

3. A four-port Ethernet (LAN) broadband router that uses one of the ports for broadband connection and the other ports for networking additional computers.

The above broadband modems are usually referred to as ADSL (Asymmetric Digital Subscriber Line) modems. Such modems allow high-speed connection to the Internet and also voice transmissions over the same telephone line. ADSL modems can be of the wired type or wireless type, with the latter being more expensive.

Other types of high-speed services which you might have come across are:

- ISDN (Integrated Services Digital Network) - a high-speed digital telephone service than enables connection to the Internet with a speed of 128 Kbps.

- Cable connection requiring a cable modem - a device that enables a broadband connection to the Internet by using cable television infrastructure with access speeds of as much as 10 Mbps.

- DSL (Digital Subscriber Line) - similar to ADSL. DSL modems can be internal or external. Internal DSL modems are plugged into an expansion slot in the computer and do not require a network adapter. External DSL modems use a network adapter to connect to the computer, therefore your PC must be network ready.

Returning to the ADSL broadband connection, you should be aware of additional limitations which do not come to light until well after you have signed up with a provider and were given or bought a modem.

For example, you need to be aware of the following facts:

If the distance between the main BT socket into your house and the extension where your computer is connected to, is greater than 10 metres, a USB connection to the broadband modem may not work - there will not be a strong enough signal for synchronisation. In that case, a broadband modem with an Ethernet connection might solve the problem, but the type 1 modem, as specified on the previous page (sometimes given to you free by your broadband supplier), may not be of much use.

If you bought a type 2 modem, as specified on the previous page, with one USB and one Ethernet connection port and you had to use the Ethernet port to connect to the broadband modem because of signal synchronisation problems, then you can not connect anything else to the Internet unless you also buy an Ethernet hub.

Therefore, it might be a good idea to research broadband modems before you commit yourself to any specific type. Find out what is available and what is more appropriate for your situation. As to the question of which make of modem you should be buying, we suggest you look up the customer reviews in such Web sites as www.amazon.co.uk before making up your mind. Try to select one with a built-in firewall.

It is also vital to find out in which country the technical support of the modem you propose to buy is based. Phone them (before you buy) and ask a general question. See if you understand the answer! Some modem manufacturers' technical support can cost you dearly as it can be charged by as much as £1.50 per minute! A very high price to pay.

Don't let us put you off broadband. You only need to browse the Web for a few hours to find out the answers to all the things we have pinpointed here. Once this is done, the rest is easy.

Installing a Broadband Modem

The first thing you have to do after connecting your new broadband modem to your computer is to install the required drivers for the particular connection. We assume here that you selected to connect your modem to your computer via the USB port, as this is the most common connection.

As most installations are Plug-and-Play, the moment you make the connection, Windows XP detects it and the message 'Found New Hardware' is displayed at the bottom right corner of your screen. The **Found New Hardware Wizard** then starts which guides you through the installation procedure of your

particular broadband modem. The same Wizard can be started manually, by clicking the **Add Hardware** icon in **Control Panel**, shown here, to display the screen in Fig. 6.15

Fig. 6.15 The New Connection Wizard.

If the modem is not recognised immediately by Windows, insert the manufacturer's CD in the CD-ROM drive and make sure the Wizard looks for the drivers on that drive. The next Wizard screen should then notify you that the USB drivers have been found and clicking **Next** proceeds with the transfer of the drivers to your hard disc.

Optionally you can connect another computer using its Ethernet port, before going on to configure your connection.

Configuring a Broadband Connection

In what follows, we assume that you have connected your broadband modem to your computer via the USB port, as this

is the most common connection. We also assume that the required drivers for the modem for this type of connection have been installed. Having done so, click the **Internet Options** icon in **Control Panel**, shown here, then click the Connections tab of the displayed Internet Properties dialogue box to open the window in Fig. 6.16.

To set up a new Internet connection, click the **Setup** button which displays the Welcome screen of the **New Connection Wizard**. Click the **Next** button, then:

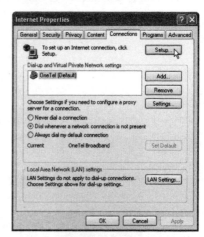

Fig. 6.16 The Internet Connections Tab-sheet.

- In the first Wizard screen, select the **Connect to the Internet** option from those available and click **Next**.

- In the second Wizard screen, select the **Set up my connection manually** option and click **Next**.

- In the third Wizard screen, select either the **Connect using a broadband connection that requires a user name and password** option or the **Connect using a broadband connection that is always on**. Which option you choose depends on your ISP. We selected the first option, then clicked **Next**.

- In the fourth Wizard screen, type the name by which you want the connection to be known.

- In the fifth Wizard screen type in your user name and password, as shown in Fig. 6.17 on the next page.

Fig. 6.17 The New Connection Wizard.

On this screen, you can select whether this account can be used by anyone using this computer, whether to make this connection the default Internet connection, or whether to turn on the Internet connection firewall. If your broadband modem incorporates a firewall, or you are using the Norton Internet Security software, you should deselect this last option.

Programs for Internet Services

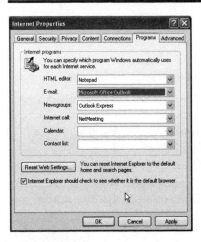

Clicking the Programs tab of the Internet Properties dialogue box displays the screen in Fig. 6.18. On this tab screen you can choose from drop-down lists which program Windows should be using automatically for Internet services such as HTML editor, E-mail, Newsgroups, Internet call, Calendar, and Contact list.

Fig. 6.18 The Internet Programs Tab-screen.

Advanced Options

You can use the Advanced tab of the Internet Properties dialogue box to select options on such diverse topics as: Accessibility, Browsing, Connection Protocols, Multimedia, Printing, Searching, and Security.

We found that these options are normally set when you customise your printer, browser, media player, etc., therefore we will not spend any more time on this tab sheet.

Publishing a File or Folder to the Web

To publish a file or folder to the Web, open **My Computer**, and navigate to the file or folder, and click the file or folder you want to publish to the Web to select it, as shown in Fig. 6.19 below.

Fig. 6.19 Selecting Folder to Publish on the Web.

Under **File and Folder Tasks**, click the **Publish this folder to the Web** link to start the **Web Publishing Wizard**. The second Wizard screen displays the contents of the folder, as shown in Fig. 6.20 on the next page, where you can select all the files or some of the files you intend to publish. Having made your selection, click the **OK** button.

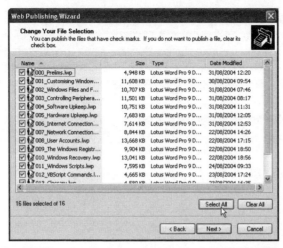

Fig. 6.20 Changing the Selection of Files to Publish on the Web.

The **Web Publishing Wizard** now initiates a connection to the internet and once you are connected the screen in Fig. 6.21 is displayed.

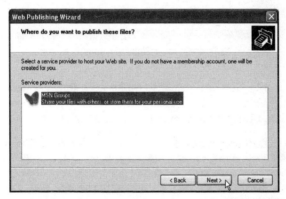

Fig. 6.21 Selecting a Service Provider to Host your Web Site.

Note that there is no option to add to the list of Service Providers who could host your Web site. If you want to publish material to your own Web site, then you must use the File Transfer Protocol (FTP) procedure, to be discussed at the end of the next chapter (page 124).

The Windows SP2 Security Centre

If you have installed Service Pack 2, you can click the **Security Center** icon in the **Control Panel**, shown here, to display the Windows Security Center screen shown in Fig. 6.22.

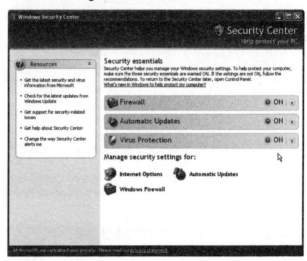

Fig. 6.22 The Windows Security Center Dialogue Box.

The Security Center's job is to make sure that Windows users are kept secure by installing the Firewall, keep Windows up-to-date at all times, and use antivirus software.

Each of these essential security components has a traffic light indicator; a green light means the security component is in place and is up-to-date, a yellow light indicates that you have disabled its monitor, and a red light means that there is a security risk and you are required to take action.

Each security component can be managed by clicking the relevant link at the bottom of the Security Center screen. We very strongly advise you to use these security components if you want to avoid malicious attacks on your computer from hackers and viruses.

7

Network Connections

A network allows several people to share the same peripherals, such as printers, scanners, and centralised backup facilities. Chances are you already have some of the hardware you will need, and you may be surprised at how easy and affordable it is to share Internet connections, and information.

Home and small business networking is very simple to install and manage, unlike the networks of large organisations. Most modern computers come network ready, which means all you need is the right type of cable to connect them together, and depending on the type of connection, you might also need a network hub. If your computer is not network enabled, then you will need to buy a network card.

Network cards come in three different architectures, and which one you choose depends on the type of slot available within your computer (you will need to open up your computer to find out). Long black slots take an ISA type card; long brown slots take an EISA type card; short white slots take a PCI type card. If you are using a laptop or notebook computer, then you could use a PCMCIA network card, the size of a credit card, which fits in a specially designed slot on your laptop.

Generally speaking there are two types of networks:

Client/Server - used by large organisations, which need to network large number of computers (between 8 and several hundred). Networked machines can either all be in the same physical area, or scattered in different places. At the centre of a client/server network is the server machine (also referred to as the file server), which has to be a much more powerful machine than the client machines (also referred to as workstations).

The server machine usually has all the programs required by users installed on its hard disc (multi-user licences are required), and can also act as a print server. As such, the server machine has to be left on at all times and, therefore, must be fitted with an Uninterruptable Power Supply and have adequate backup facilities. Obviously, setting up and running such a network requires specialist knowledge and is normally carried out by a Network Administrator.

Peer-to-Peer - used by home and small businesses, which only require to network a small number of computers (up to 8). The most popular connection method is called Ethernet, but its drawback is the need to run wires from computer to computer. You can run up to 90 metres of special wire with little data slowdown. At 100 megabits per second (Mbps), Ethernet is easily fast enough to handle a broadband Internet connection and still move plenty of local data.

The other option of connecting peer-to-peer computers is wireless. There are two popular options; the 802.11b (also known as 'Wi-Fi'), and the Bluetooth wireless technology. A wireless network is usually easier to install than an Ethernet network, but configuring the equipment can take a little longer. The speed of a wireless network is generally faster than a broadband connection, therefore you will not notice any slowdown even when large files are being transferred across the network.

Lately there has been an upgrade to the 802.11b standard, namely the 802.11a, which operates at 5 GHz with a throughput of five times that of the 802.11b, but is rather expensive to buy. The latest entrant to these standards is the 802.11g which splits the difference in throughput between the other two standards, and is cheaper than the 802.11a.

With a peer-to-peer network, there is no centralised server machine; all computers on the network have equal status. Also, you don't need special software to run the network. Everything you need comes with Windows XP, and is very easy to implement. There is even a **Network Setup Wizard** to help you with the job at hand.

Using the Network Setup Wizard

If you have installed the Windows Service Pack 2, you can

start the **Network Setup Wizard** by double-clicking
the additional **Control Panel** icon, shown here.

If you have not installed Service Pack 2, you can
still start the **Network Setup Wizard**, but in a
slightly roundabout way. First, click the **Network
Connections** icon in the **Control Panel**, shown
here, to open the Network Connections screen
shown in Fig. 7.1 below. To see a similar view to
the one below, select the option **List** in the **View** sub-menu.

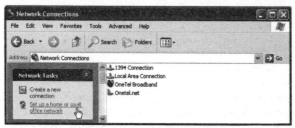

Fig. 7.1 The Network Connections Screen.

Next, click the **Set up a home or small office network** link to
start the **Network Setup Wizard**, as shown in Fig. 7.2.

Fig. 7.2 The Network Setup Wizard.

To proceed with the Wizard, click the **Next** button and do the following:

*   In the first Wizard screen, click the **checklist for creating a network** link, as shown in Fig. 7.3

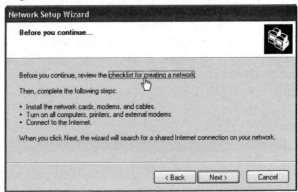

Fig. 7.3 The First Network Setup Wizard Screen.

This activates the **Help and Support Center** and gives you a detailed screen on the steps you need to take to create a home or small office network. We suggest that you spend some time with this help screen.

*   In the second Wizard screen, select the Internet connection from the displayed list through which you would like to access the Internet, then click **Next**. Obviously, you need to have set up such a connection before it will appear in the list.

*   In the third Wizard screen, select the option that best describes your computer in terms of connectivity, then click the **Next** button.

*   In the fourth Wizard screens, type in a computer name by which your computer will be known, such as 'Study PC', etc., while in the fifth Wizard screen, provide a working group name, such as Home or Office.

*   In the sixth Wizard screen (SP2 only), you are asked whether or not you want to establish file and printer sharing.

- In the next Wizard screen, you are given a summary of the settings the Wizard will apply, as shown in Fig. 7.4; it might take a few seconds to do so.

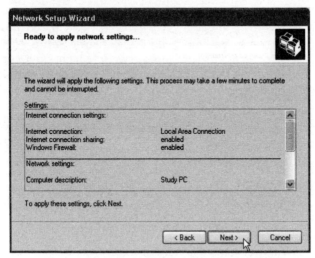

Fig. 7.4 The Network Setup Wizard Summary Screen.

- In the next Wizard screen computers are shown in an animated graphical display in the process of being connected to a group, as shown in Fig. 7.5 below.

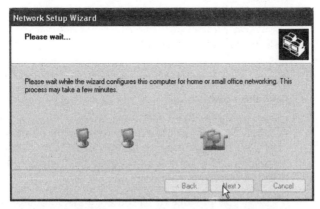

Fig. 7.5 Part of the animated Network Setup Wizard Screen.

At this stage, the Wizard under Service Pack 2, asks you to restart your computer so that all changes can take effect. Pre SP2 users have a few more steps to get through, as follows:

*   In the next Wizard screen, shown in Fig. 7.6, you are given information on what you need to do next. For example, you must run the **Network Setup Wizard** on all computers on the network which operate under Windows XP, or create a Network Setup disc to be run on computers which do not operate under Windows XP.

Fig. 7.6 The Eighth Network Setup Wizard Screen.

Obviously, there are one or two other choices available to you on this Wizard screen.

*   In the last Wizard screen, shown in Fig. 7.7 on the next page, you are given two links to the Help and Support Center. The first link provides information on how to use the Shared Documents folder, while the second link gives you an overview on shared files and folders. It is worth pursuing both these links.

*   Finally, you are asked to restart your computer so that all the settings take effect.

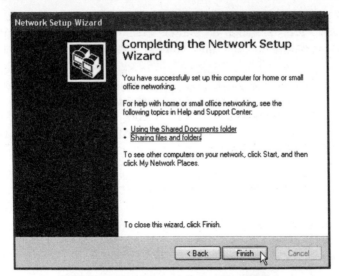

Fig. 7.7 The Final Network Setup Wizard Screen.

As you can see, connecting your computers to a home or small office network is very easy to do, particularly with SP2. All that remains is to arrange for certain files and folders to be shared.

Sharing Information and Hardware

You can share files and folders stored on your computer, on a network, and on the Web. The method you choose for sharing information depends on whom you want to share it with and what computer they will use to access it. There are three main categories:

- Everyone who uses your computer can share information by using 'Shared folders' which are counterparts to your personal folders, such as My Documents, with its sub-folders My Pictures, and My Music. Shared Documents, with its sub-folders Shared Pictures, and Shared Music provide a place for you to store files, pictures, and music that can be accessed by all users of your computer.

- You can also share information and resources, such as a disc, folder or printer, between computers on the same network and control whether the files on the shared folder can be modified by other users.

- Finally, you can share your files online by publishing them on the Web in a private folder that you control.

In what follows, we will examine in turn how you can achieve sharing under each category.

Sharing Folders and Files on your PC

To share a folder with other users of the same computer, first locate it (ours is a sub-folder in **My Documents** folder), select it and drag it to the **Shared Documents** link in **Other Places**. The folder will then be moved from its present position to within the **Shared Documents** folder.

If you want to make a copy of the folder rather than move it, hold down the <Ctrl> key while dragging. You will be able to tell that the intended move will copy the folder by the display of the small

Fig. 7.8 Drag-copying a Folder.

plus (+) sign next to the mouse pointer, as shown in Fig. 7.8. When you release the mouse button a small dialogue box appears at the top-left of your screen, as shown here. To start the copying process, you must click the **Copy Here** entry which then displays the copying box shown in Fig. 7.9.

Fig. 7.9 The Copying Information Box.

To move or copy a file into the **Shared Documents** folder, select the file and click either the **Move this file** or the **Copy this file** link. This opens the Move Items (or Copy Items) screen in which you select into which sub-folder in the **Shared Documents** you want to move or copy your selected file.

Fig. 7.10 The Internet Programs Screen.

It is a good idea to always move or copy an item into a meaningful sub-folder rather than moving or copying files into the main **Shared Documents** folder. If such a sub-folder does not exist, create it by using the **Make New Folder** button, while the **Shared Documents** folder is selected. The created folder will always be created within the folder you highlight in the Move or Copy dialogue box. To complete the Move or Copy command, select the sub-folder into which you

Fig. 7.11 The Move Items Screen.

want to place your file and click the **Move** (or **Copy**) button on the dialogue box in Fig. 7.11. As you can also see, the two folders, **Shared Music**, and **Shared Pictures** were created by Windows XP during installation for your convenience.

If you now use **My Computer** and open the **Shared Documents** folder, you will find the file you chose to share inside the newly created sub-folder.

Sharing a Drive or Folder on the Network

If you are connected to a network, you can share a drive or folder on your computer with others connected to the network. To start the process, you must log on as the administrator, then:

- Use **My Computer**, and right-click the drive you want to share, and click the **Sharing and Security** option from the drop-down menu, as shown in Fig. 7.12 below.

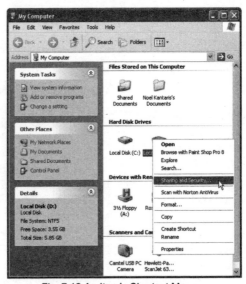

Fig. 7.12 An Item's Shortcut Menu.

- On the Sharing tab of the displayed dialogue box, click the **If you understand the risk but still want to share the root of the drive, click here** link.

- On the displayed screen, shown in Fig. 7.13 on the next page, you now have the option of allowing the sharing of the selected folder (drive D: in our case) with other users on the network, by clicking the **Share this folder on the network** check box. The letter D appears automatically in the **Share name** text box.

- To change the name of the folder on the network, type a new name in the **Share name** text box. This does not change the name of the original folder on your computer.

- If the **Share this folder on the network** check box is not available to you, then either your computer is not connected to the network, or you are not logged in as the administrator of this computer.

- To share a single folder with other users on the network, follow the same procedure as explained above, but this time right-click the folder you want to share

Fig. 7.13 The Sharing Properties Screen.

Fig. 7.14 The Sharing Folder Screen.

instead of right-clicking a whole drive. Windows will jump straight to the dialogue box shown in Fig. 7.14, without opening the warning box in Fig. 7.13.

- In the dialogue box in Fig. 7.14 you have the option to allow or disallow network users to change your files by selecting or deselecting the appropriate check box. Think hard before allowing anyone to change your files!

Sharing your Printer

If you are connected to a network, you can share a printer on your computer with others connected to the network. Printers are not shared by default when you install them on Windows XP Home edition. To start the process of sharing a printer, you must log on as the administrator, then:

- Click the *start* menu command **Printers and Faxes**.

- On the displayed Printers and Faxes dialogue box, right-click the printer you want to share and select **Sharing** on the drop-down menu shown in Fig. 7.15 to display the Printer's Properties Sharing screen (Fig. 7.16).

Fig. 7.15 The Printers and Faxes Dialogue Box.

- The options you see on the Sharing tab differ depending whether 'sharing' is enabled. If you see a message stating that printer sharing must be turned on, you must run the **Network Setup Wizard** which can be started by clicking the link on the Sharing tab.

- If the **Share this printer** option appears on the screen, as in Fig. 7.16, type in a name for the shared printer and click the **OK** button.

Fig. 7.16 The Printer's Sharing Properties Screen.

File and Folder Permissions

If you are connected to a network, you can set, view, change, or remove file and folder permissions for a drive or folder on your computer which you share with others connected to the network. However, you can only set file and folder permissions on drives formatted to use NTFS - the advanced file system that includes features not found in any version of FAT. To change permissions you must be the owner of the file or folder, or be the administrator of the system. Then do the following:

- Use **My Computer** to locate, then select and right-click the shared file or folder, and click the **Properties** option from the drop-down menu, as shown in Fig. 7.17 below.

Fig. 7.17 An Item's Shortcut Menu.

- On the displayed dialogue box, click the Security tab. If you are using NTFS and the Security tab does not appear on the Properties dialogue box, then do the following:

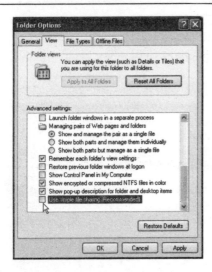

Click *start*, **Control Panel**, **Appearance and Themes**, and then click **Folder Options**.

On the **View** tab, under **Advanced settings**, clear **Use simple file sharing (Recommended)**, shown in Fig. 7.18.

Fig. 7.18 The View Folder Options Screen.

My Network Places

You can use this option on the *start* menu to gain access to and get information on files and folders on other computers on a network. You can also use this facility to send files and folders to a Web site using FTP by doing the following:

- Use the *start*, **My Network Places** menu command which displays the screen in Fig. 7.19 below.

Fig. 7.19 The My Network Places Screen.

- Click the **Add a network place** link under **Network Tasks** to start the **Add Network Place Wizard**, which helps you sign up for a service that offers online storage space, such as your Web site host.

- On the second Wizard screen, shown in Fig. 7.20 below, type in the Internet or network address. Examples are displayed on the Wizard screen, as shown below, by clicking the appropriate link.

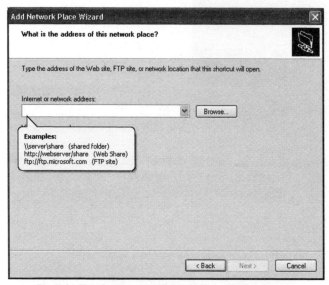

Fig. 7.20 The Second Add Network Place Wizard Screen.

What you type in the **Internet or network address** text box for uploading files using FTP should have been given to you by your Web site host. If it is a network address you are entering, then look at the examples above, or consult your network administrator.

- On the third Wizard screen, you are asked to provide a suitable name for the connection which will appear in **My Network Places**, and can be anything you like. After typing it in, click the **Next** button to take you to the final Wizard screen, shown in Fig. 7.21 on the next page.

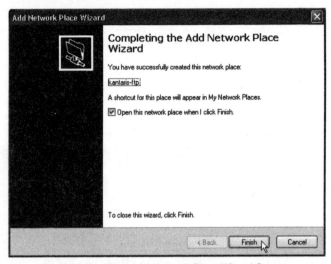

Fig. 7.21 The Final Add Network Place Wizard Screen.

- If the **Open this network place when I click Finish** is checked, the Wizard connects you to the specified address when you click the **Finish** button.

In future, when you want to connect to the network place, use the *start*, **My Network Places** menu command and double-click the required entry, as shown in Fig. 7.22 below.

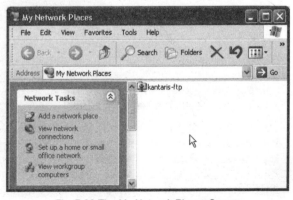

Fig. 7.22 The My Network Places Screen.

8

User Accounts

In this chapter we will examine how you can create and

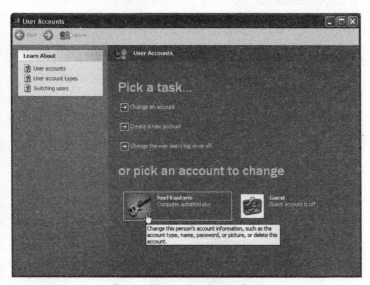

change user accounts settings and passwords, and how to increase security on your PC. We begin by double-clicking the **User Accounts** icon on the **Control Panel**, shown here, to display the

screen in Fig. 8.1 in Classic View.

The Computer Administrator

In the User Accounts screen, shown below, click the **Computer administrator** link under the **or pick an account to change** entry to display the screen in Fig. 8.2.

Fig. 8.1 The User Accounts Screen.

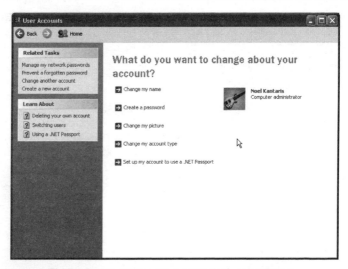

Fig. 8.2 The Computer Administrator's Account Screen.

Obviously you need to log on as the computer's administrator before most of the options on the administrator account screen can be accessed or acted upon. From here, you can change your name, change the picture representing you (see pages 3 and 131), or create a password, as shown in Fig. 8.3 below.

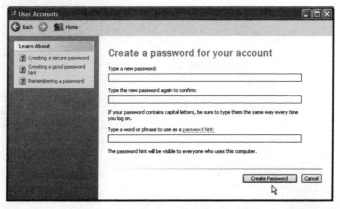

Fig. 8.3 Creating a Password for your Account.

Do have a look at the topics listed under **Learn About** on the left panel of the screen in Fig. 8.3. It is worth finding out how to create a secure password and how to remember it. Another option in Fig. 8.2 allows you to change the account type, as shown in Fig. 8.4 below.

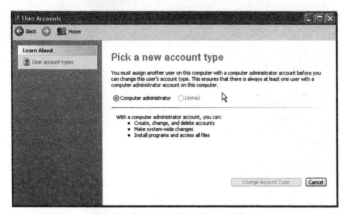

Fig. 8.4 Picking a New Account Type.

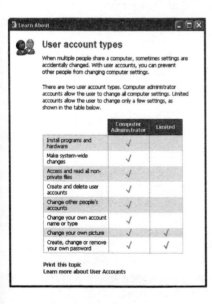

As you can see, you must assign another user on this computer with an administrator's privileges before you can change the currently logged in user's account to a different type. This is to ensure that this computer has at least one administrator. In Fig. 8.5, we display the screen you will get if you click the link under **Learn About** in Fig. 8.4.

Fig. 8.5 User Account Types.

This screen can also be opened by clicking the second link under **Learn About** in Fig. 8.1. The other two links on this screen display information on 'User accounts' and 'Switching users', as shown in Fig. 8.6 and Fig. 8.7 below.

Fig. 8.6 The User Accounts Help Screen.

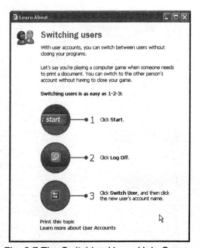

Fig. 8.7 The Switching Users Help Screen.

Obviously, before you can switch between users you must first create their accounts, as we shall see next.

Creating a New Account

If more than one person is to use your computer, then you may want to create an account for each person. Windows XP allows each user on your computer the means of customising their account to their own requirements. For example, they can customise their desktop, and they can customise the way windows display on screen.

Each user also benefits from having their own documents folder so their personal files are kept separate from those of other users, they have separate Internet settings, separate favourites and separate e-mail folders. Individual users can also password protect their accounts so everyone can feel safe in the knowledge that their individualised settings will not be changed by accident or intent. Most definitely, the computer administrators should password protect their accounts.

To create a new user account do the following:

* Log on as the administrator, then use the *start*, **Control Panel** menu command and double-click the **User Accounts** icon. In the displayed window, shown in Fig. 8.8 below, click the **Create a new account** link under the **Pick a task** entry.

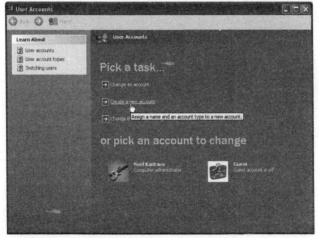

Fig. 8.8 Creating a New Account.

- In the displayed 'Name the new account' window, shown in Fig. 8.9, type in the name of the new account holder and click the **Next** button.

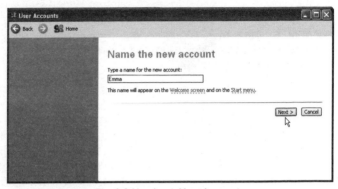

Fig. 8.9 Naming a New Account.

- If the person in question is too young, it might be a good idea to select **Limited** as the account type, as shown in Fig. 8.10, and click the **Create Account** button.

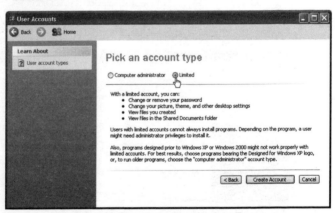

Fig. 8.10 Selecting a New Account Type.

- On the next displayed window, shown in Fig. 8.11 on the next page, click on the newly created account under the **or pick an account to change**.

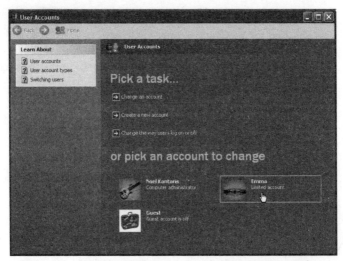

Fig. 8.11 Picking an Account to Change.

• On the displayed 'What do you want to change' window, shown in Fig. 8.12 below, click the **Change the picture** link (pointed to).

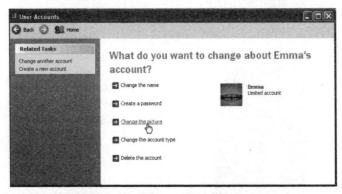

Fig. 8.12 Changing an Account Picture.

• In the displayed 'Pick a picture' window, shown in Fig. 8.13 on the next page, select an appropriate picture and click the **Change Picture** button.

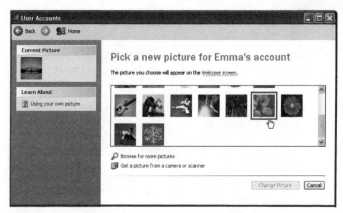

Fig. 8.13 Selecting an Account Picture.

- Next, the window of Fig. 8.12 is displayed once more where you can **Create a password** or click the **Home** Toolbar button to return to the 'Welcome screen' shown in Fig. 8.14 below.

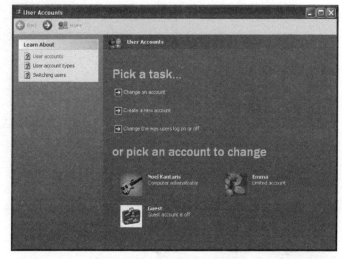

Fig. 8.14 The New Welcome Screen.

Switching Accounts

In Windows XP there are two simple ways of switching users without having to restart the computer. However, if you are using Offline Files, you can only switch users by using the *start*, **Log Off** command and restarting the computer.

To use Fast Switching, you will have to disable the Offline Files option as follows:

- Log on as the administrator, then use the *start*, **Control Panel** menu command and in the displayed **User Accounts** screen, shown in Fig. 8.15, click the **Change the way users log on or off** link (pointed to) under the **Pick a task** entry.

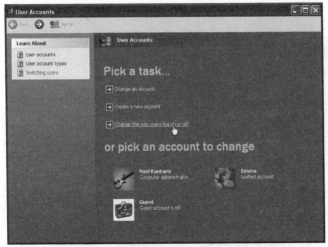

Fig. 8.15 Changing the Way Users Log On or Off.

- On the displayed Offline Files Settings dialogue box, remove the check mark from the **Enable Offline Files** box, then click the **Apply** button followed by the **OK** button.

- On the next window to open, shown in Fig. 8.16, select the **Use fast user switching** option and click the **Apply Options** button.

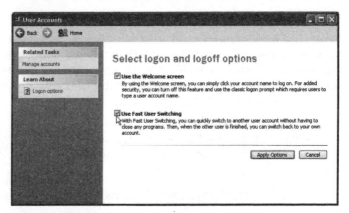

Fig. 8.16 Selecting Log On and Log Off Options.

Now using the *start*, **Log Off** command displays the box shown in Fig. 8.17 below. Clicking the **Switch User** option

Fig. 8.17 The Log Off
Windows box.

displays the Welcome screen shown in Fig. 8.18, showing all the users of the computer so that you can select one.

A faster method of getting to the Welcome screen is by pressing the **Windows logo** (🪟) and **L** keys together.

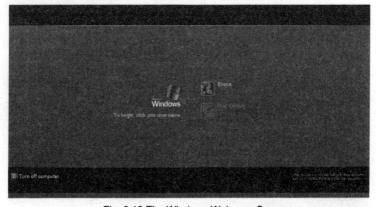

Fig. 8.18 The Windows Welcome Screen.

Using an E-mail Program

When the newly created user first attempts to use the e-mail facilities provided by, say, Outlook Express, the first screen of the **Internet Connection Wizard**, shown in Fig 8.19 below, is displayed. In this and subsequent screens you need to provide the new user's e-mail connection details.

If the Wizard does not open, or if you want to change your connection details, use the **Tools**, **Accounts** menu command in Outlook Express, select the mail tab and click the **Add** button and select **Mail**.

Fig. 8.19 The First Internet Connection Wizard Screen.

In the first screen of the Wizard, type the user's name in the text box, shown above, and click the **Next** button to display the second screen, shown in Fig. 8.20 on the next page. Enter their e-mail address in the text box, if they have not organised one yet you could always sign up for free e-mail with Hotmail (see the extreme right column of the screen dump in Fig. 8.24). Hotmail is a free browser-based e-mail service owned by Microsoft.

In the third Wizard screen enter the e-mail server details, as shown for us in Fig. 8.21, also on the next page. To complete some of the details here you may need to ask your e-mail provider, or your system administrator, for help.

Fig. 8.20 The Second Internet Connection Wizard Screen.

The details given here must be unique to the specified user, and should be different from those of other users of this PC, otherwise you might receive e-mail not intended for your eyes!

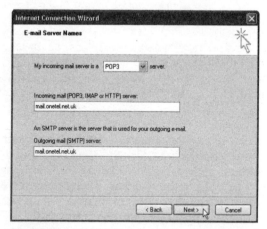

Fig. 8.21 The Third Internet Connection Wizard Screen.

The next Wizard screen asks for a user name and password. Both these would have been given by your e-mail provider. Type these in, as shown here in Fig. 8.22 on the next page, and click the **Next** button.

If you select the **Remember password** option in this box, you
will not have to enter these details every time you log on. **BUT**
it may not be wise to do this if your PC is in a busy office - for
obvious security reasons.

Fig. 8.22 The Fourth Internet Connection Wizard Screen.

This leads to the final Wizard screen informing you of your
success, which completes the procedure, so press **Finish** to
return you to the Network Connections dialogue box, asking
you to select a connection. These connections to the Internet
via an Internet Service Provider (ISP), are the same for all
users of this PC and were first established by the computer's
administrator.

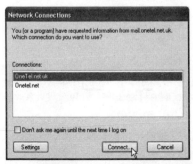

Fig. 8.23 The Internet Accounts Dialogue Box.

Once a connection is established, you can click the Read Mail coloured link, or the **Inbox** entry in the Folder List on the left side of the Outlook Express opening window. Both of these actions open the Inbox, which when opened for the first time, will probably contain a message from Microsoft, like that shown in Fig. 8.24 below.

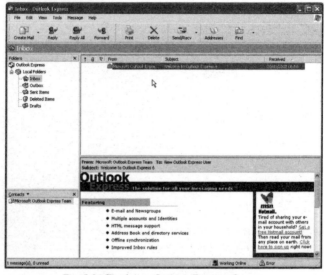

Fig. 8.24 The Inbox Outlook Express Screen.

This shows the default Outlook Express Main window layout, which consists of a Folders List to the left with a Contacts List (from the Address Book) below it, a Message List to the right and a Preview Pane below that. The list under Folders contains all the active mail folders, news servers and newsgroups.

Clicking on one of these displays its contents in the Message List, and clicking on a message opens a Preview of it below for you to see. Double-clicking on a message opens the message in its own window.

If you want to know more about Outlook Express, may we suggest you have a look at our book *Internet Explorer 6 and Outlook Express 6 explained* (BP513), also published by Bernard Babani (publishing) Ltd.

Activating the Guest Account

You can provide limited computer access to guests to your home who might require to look at and process their e-mail, by activating the Guest account. To do so, however, you must log on as the computer administrator, and then on the User Accounts window click the Guest icon as shown in Fig. 8.25.

Fig. 8.25 Activating the Guest Account.

This opens the screen shown in Fig. 8.26 below in which you click the **Turn On the Guest Account** button.

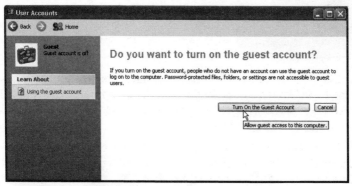

Fig. 8.26 Turning on the Guest Account.

As with other users of this computer, a Guest account needs information about the person's e-mail provider, as discussed previously. An alternative option would be for the guest to use the Microsoft Hotmail facility, but to do so they must be online. Whichever e-mail facility you choose, as a Guest user you cannot connect to the Internet - they must get another user of this computer to first connect to the Internet before they can proceed. The same applies to disconnecting from the Internet after use.

As mentioned earlier (and when connected to the Internet), clicking the **Get a free Hotmail account** link at the extreme right column of the Outlook Express Inbox screen (see Fig. 8.24), displays the screen in Fig. 8.27 below.

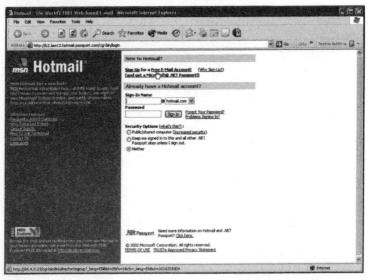

Fig. 8.27 The MSN Hotmail Sign-in Screen.

The same screen can be displayed by starting Internet Explorer and typing www.hotmail.com in the address box. From here you can either sign up for a free e-mail account or sign-in, if you already have an account established. One word of caution; you must use a newly signed up account within 10 days after it becomes activated, and after that you must use it at least once every 30 days if the account is not to be lost.

Increasing Computer Security

You can increase your computer's security by first disabling fast switching between users. To do so, log on as the computer's administrator, log off all other users by switching to their account and using the *start*, **Log Off** command, then do the following:

- Use the *start*, **Control Panel** menu command and click the **User Accounts** button. On the displayed screen click the **Change the way users log on or off** link.

- In the displayed 'Select logon and logoff options' screen, shown in Fig. 8.28, click the **Logon options** link under the **Learn About** entry on the left panel of the screen.

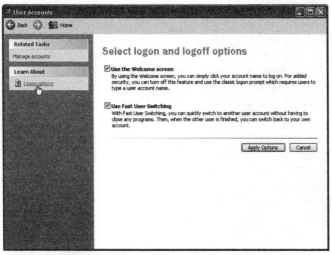

Fig. 8.28 Selecting Log On and Log Off Options.

- The displayed screen, shown in Fig. 8.29 on the next page, contains information on what happens when either or both of the check marks in Fig. 8.28 are removed.

Fig. 8.29 The Learn About
Log-on Options Screen.

Obviously, disabling the Fast User Switching option adds a bit more security to the system and allows you to use Offline Files, but it still retains the friendly way of logging in, as it allows you to click your name on the Welcome screen and type a password, if you have one, to log on.

However, if Fast User Switching is disabled, using the **Windows Logo** (⌨) and **L** keys together, locks the computer and only the administrator of the PC can unlock it. Also the Guest user is barred from browsing the Web or using any e-mail facility, because when a user who has access to the Internet logs off, the connection is shut down automatically.

If now, in addition to disabling the Fast User Switching option, you also disable the Welcome screen option, you increase security even more as you eliminate the possibility of a Trojan horse (a rogue program that collects information from your computer) disguising as a system log-on and retrieving user names and passwords that the writers of the Trojan horse can later use to break into your system when you are connected to the Internet.

In other words, increasing security decreases convenience of use of your computer, and vice versa. The choice is yours to make!

9

The Windows Registry

The Microsoft Windows XP Registry is a hierarchical database in which the operating system stores most of its settings. For example, it defines how the operating system starts, how the Start menu and Taskbar work, and what you see on the Desktop, to mention but a few of the operating system's user interface. It also contains information about what hardware is installed on the system, such as printers, modem, scanner, etc., and the ports that are being used.

The Registry is also where programs store their settings. It is continually referenced during operations, such as determining profiles for each user, the applications installed on the computer and the types of documents that each user can access or create, and holds information on file associations, the settings for folders and application icons.

A lot of the Registry entries are changed automatically when you change settings in the Control Panel. Such changes take place behind the scene, so to speak, and you don't need to know anything about either the Registry itself or how to edit it directly. This is mostly referred to as the software method of changing the Registry.

Some badly behaved software can add entries to the Registry which can change the smooth operation of your computer in which case restoring your PC to an earlier Restore point might eliminate the problem. Other software, when uninstalled, tend to leave entries in the Registry which bloats it and slows down your computer's operations. It is in such cases that learning how to change settings in the Registry directly can improve the performance of your PC and enhance your knowledge of Windows XP. However, changing the Registry directly is very dangerous unless you have a valid backup of it and you know how to restore it correctly.

The Windows XP Registry Structure

At this stage we will just take a quick look at the Registry, but be very careful not to change anything - not until you learn how to Backup and Restore it, which we will cover shortly. If you are tempted to change anything without knowing exactly what you are doing, you may well make your computer unusable, so **be warned!**

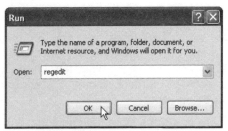

To have a look at the Registry and see its structure, use the *start*, **Run** command, and type **regedit** in the **Open** box of the displayed dialogue box as shown in Fig. 9.1.

Fig. 9.1 The Open Dialogue Box.

Clicking the **OK** button displays the Registry Editor Screen shown in Fig. 9.2 below.

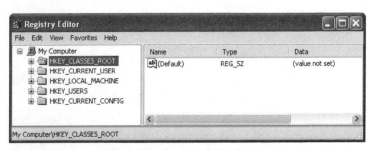

Fig. 9.2 The Registry Editor Screen.

The Registry Editor **regedit.exe** is an executable file (an application program) supplied by Microsoft so that you can use it to view and change the values held in the Registry. The editor's interface is similar to that of the Explorer with two panes, with the left pane displaying the five root keys. Each key can be expanded using the plus (+) icon to display its contents, then collapsed using the minus (-) icon (see Fig. 9.3).

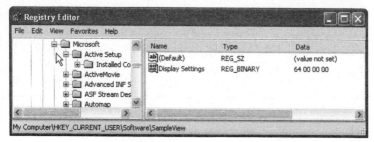

Fig. 9.3 Expanding and Collapsing Registry Keys.

As seen above, the left pane of the Registry Editor behaves in a similar way to the folders pane of the Explorer, but instead of expanding and collapsing folders, it does the same thing to the contents of each of the five root Registry keys, including their sub-keys. The path of a selected item is displayed on the bottom-left corner of the Registry Editor.

In Windows XP there are five root (top or main) keys (see Fig. 9.2), each containing a specific portion of the information stored in the Registry and starting with the letters HKEY. These are:

* *HKEY_CLASSES_ROOT* – contains all your file types as well as Object Linking and Embedding (OLE) information for all your OLE-aware applications.

* *HKEY_CURRENT_USER* – points to the part of HKEY_USERS appropriate for the current user.

* *HKEY_LOCAL_MACHINE* – contains information about all of the hardware and software installed on your computer.

* *HKEY_USERS* – contains certain preferences (such as colours and control panel settings) for each of the users of the computer. In Windows XP, the default key contains a template to be used for newly-added users.

* *HKEY_CURRENT_CONFIG* – specifies the current hardware configuration, as it is possible to have more than one hardware configuration.

The right pane of the Registry Editor, however, differs to that of the Explorer in that it does not display files but individual items called *values*. Every value has a name and is capable of holding one of several types of data. Furthermore, every key contains a value named *(default)* and if it does not contain any data, it is displayed as *(value not set)*, as shown in both Figs 9.2 & 9.3.

The value types of the Registry are listed below. Each value has a common name and a symbolic name, shown in parentheses in the following list.

- *String Values* (REG_SZ) – they contain strings of characters (text). They are of prime interest to us here because they display in plain English and are easy to understand and edit.

- *String Array Values* (REG_MULTI_SZ) – they contain concatenated strings. Each character within a string is separated by a single null character (ASCII code 00), while multiple strings are separated by three null characters in a row. Such values cannot be created in the Registry Editor, but can be edited.

- *Expanded Sring Value*s (REG_EXPAND_SZ) – they contain variables, such as %SystemRoot%, into which Windows substitutes information, such as c:\windows\, before handing it over to the owning application. Such values cannot be created in the Registry Editor, but can be edited.

- *Binary Values* (REG_BINARY) – they contain data in hexadecimal code in which each individual character is specified by a two-digit number in a base-16 number system represented by the digits 0 through 9 and the letters A (equivalent to decimal 10) through F (equivalent to decimal 15).

- *DWORD Values* (REG_DWORD) – they contain a number, such as 0 for 'no' and 1 for 'yes'. The DWORD format, like the binary one, is a hexadecimal number but in an easier representation.

Backing up the Registry

Before you do anything to the Registry (apart from just looking), you must learn how to make a valid backup and, if things go wrong, know how to restore it.

There are two distinctive ways of backing up the Registry, depending on your requirements and storage capabilities. If you are backing up the whole Registry, use the Windows Backup utility, while if you are backing up a Registry hive (such as *HKEY_USERS*), or single key, use the Export method.

Backing up the Whole Registry

To back up the whole Registry, use the Windows Backup utility to back up the System State - the Registry, with its main five keys and all their sub-keys, the COM+ Class Registration Database, files under Windows File Protection, and boot files.

As discussed on page 70, but repeated here for the sake of completeness, Windows XP comes with a Backup Utility which is installed by default in the Professional Edition, but has to be installed manually in the Home Edition. The Backup utility is included on the Windows XP Home Edition CD-ROM in the ValueAdd folder, but it does not support the **Automated System Recovery Wizard**.

To manually install Backup, double-click the NTBackup.msi file in the

        e:\ValueAdd\msft\NTBackup

location on the Windows XP Home Edition CD, where e: is our CD-ROM drive (yours might be different). Next, follow the instructions of the Wizard and when installation is complete, click **Finish**.

The Backup utility is accessible via the *start*, **All Programs**, **Accessories**, **System Tools** cascade menu. On the first screen of the **Backup or Restore Wizard**, click the **Advanced mode** link shown in Fig. 9.4 on the next page. This displays the Welcome screen of the Advanced Mode Backup Utility shown in Fig. 9.5, also on the next page.

Fig. 9.4 The Backup or Restore Wizard.

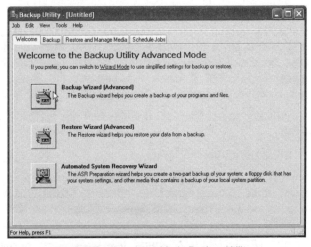

Fig. 9.5 The Advanced Mode Backup Utility.

Clicking the **Backup Wizard** (Advanced) button, pointed to in Fig. 9.5, displays the first screen of the **Advanced Backup Wizard** which has a setting to back up the System State either to one of the hard drives or to a different media of your choice.

If the registry does become corrupt, the System State backup is used to restore the system. If you are using the Professional Edition of Windows XP, you can use the **Automated System Recovery Wizard** button to help you create a two-part backup of your system. However, this facility is not supported in the Windows XP Home Edition.

Continuing with the **Advanced Backup Wizard** method, select the **Only backup the System State data** option and click the **Next** button to display the third Wizard screen in which you can choose the place were you want to save your backup and what name to give it (you could even choose to save it on 3½″ floppy discs!). We chose an external hard drive F: and called our file **System State Backup**. Clicking the **Next** button, displays the final Wizard screen shown in Fig. 9.6.

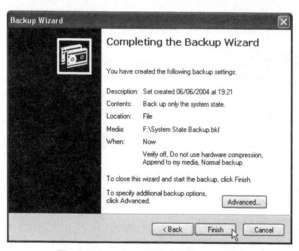

Fig. 9.6 The Final Backup Wizard Screen.

Clicking the **Finish** button, starts the backup as shown in Fig. 9.7 on the next page.

As you can see, in less than 2 minutes the whole System State was backed up. It could not be easier. Furthermore, since the actual size of the backup file is less than 380 MB, you could have used your CD-ROM writer to burn it onto a CD.

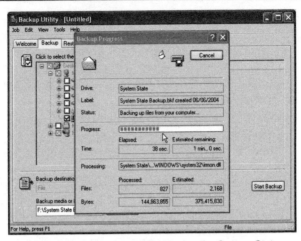

Fig. 9.7 In the Process of Backing up the System State.

Restoring a System State Backup

To restore the whole Registry from a backup file, locate it on the media you used to save it, and double-click it. This starts the **Restore Wizard**, the third screen of which is shown in Fig. 9.8. To start the process, you must select the actual System State file, as shown below, before clicking **Next**.

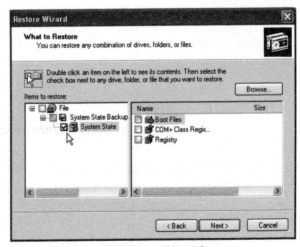

Fig. 9.8 The Restore Wizard Screen.

Exporting a Registry Hive or Single Key

To export a Registry hive or a single key, follow the procedure outlined below.

*   Use the **start**, **Run** command, type **regedit** in the **Open** box of the displayed dialogue box, and click **OK**.

*   Locate and then click the key that contains the value that you want to edit (either an entire hive, as shown in Fig. 9.9, or a single key).

Fig. 9.9 The Restore Wizard Screen.

*   On the **File** menu, click **Export**.

*   In the **Save in** box, select a location where you want to save the Registration Entries, and in the **Save as type** drop-down selection box select the **.reg** file type. Finally, in the **File name** box, type a file name, click the **All** radio button, and click **Save**, as shown in Fig. 9.10 on the next page.

Note the two radio buttons **All** and **Selected branch** which are used in the following circumstances:

*   To copy the entire Registry tree, select **All**.

*   To copy only the key selected in the Registry and all branches below it, click **Selected branches**.

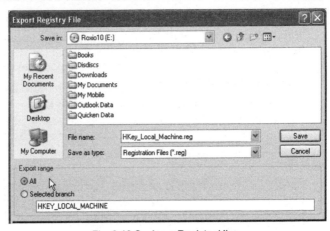

Fig. 9.10 Saving a Registry Hive.

The available file types can be seen by clicking the down-arrow to the right of the **Save as type** box, as shown here. The significance of these file types and their use is explained below.

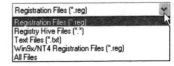

- The Registration Files option creates a **.reg** file which can be read and edited either within Notepad as a text file, or directly using the Registry Editor. Once changes have been made and saved within Notepad, right clicking the file and using the **Merge** command adds the changed file back into the registry. However, any *additions* made to the registry using **regedit** prior to merging, will not be removed.

- The Registry Hive Files option creates a binary image of the selected registry key. Such an image file cannot be viewed or edited in Notepad or any other text editor. The purpose of such a file is to allow you to import it back into the registry to ensure any problematic changes you made are eliminated.

- The Text Files option creates a text file containing the information in the selected key. Its most useful purpose is creating a snapshot of a key that you can refer back to if necessary. It cannot be merged back into the registry like a Registration File.

- The Win9x/NT4 Registration Files option creates a **.reg** file in the same manner used by the Registration Files option. It is only used if you want to merge a key from XP into a previous version of Windows.

Obviously, the most effective and safest method of backing up the registry is to use the Registry Hive Files option. No matter what goes wrong in your editing, importing the image of the key will remove all problematic changes or additions.

Restoring a .REG File Backup

We have already mentioned that a **.reg** file can be restored by navigating to where it is stored, right-clicking it and selecting **Merge** from the drop-down menu. Another option on the same menu is the **Open With** command which displays the Open With dialogue box with the Registry Editor selected. Both these restoring options are also available from the **File** menu when the **.reg** file is selected.

Whichever of the above methods you action, a warning box will be displayed asking you whether you really want the contents of the file to be merged with the equivalent Registry key. The same warning box appears if you double-click the **.reg** file, so take care with your response!

The final method of restoring a **.reg** file is from the Registry Editor menu bar using the **File**, **Import** command, then navigating to where the **.reg** file is saved, selecting the file and clicking **Open**. The contents of the **.reg** file will be merged into the current registry followed by a confirmation dialogue box informing you of the successful outcome! Although this method forces you to consciously select the **.reg** file you want to import, you must be extra careful to select the correct **.reg** file - there is no warning if you don't!

Editing a Registry Key

Now that you have hopefully learned how to back up and restore a Registry key, it is safe to start experimenting with editing - but back up first!

Warning: Using the Registry Editor incorrectly can seriously damage your operating system which might require you to reinstall it. Even Microsoft cannot guarantee that problems resulting from incorrectly editing the Registry can be solved. If you find yourself in a situation in which Windows refuses to start up and you have a valid backup of your Registry, please refer to Chapter 10, before reinstalling Windows.

We hope you are still courageous enough to follow us in our exploration of the Registry. We had to present you with the worst possible scenario in case you are the one person who might be tempted to start changing values in the Registry without having a valid Registry backup.

Some Editing Examples

1. Changing the Registered Owner
When you first used Setup to install Windows XP, you were asked to enter your name and Company name. Like most people we gave our name and typed "Home PC" for the Company name. This information is then assigned by Windows to the Registered Owner of the PC and used by other installed programs for registering purposes. To see this information, use the *start*, **Control Panel** menu command and double-click the **System** icon which displays the System Properties dialogue box with its General tab selected. This screen is shown for one of our computers in Fig. 9.11 on the next page.

The Registered owner and Company details, as shown, cannot be changed from within Windows, but you can change them in the Registry. You might be selling your computer and you don't want your name to remain on the PC, or you might even want to impress the person who is buying your computer by changing the registered name to theirs!

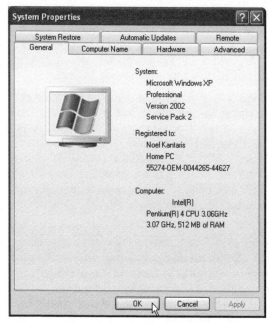

Fig. 9.11 The System Properties Dialogue box.

To change the Registered owner and Company name, you need to open the Registry Editor and navigate to:

HKEY_LOCAL_MACHINE\SOFTWARE\Microsoft\Windows NT\CurrentVersion

The values you need to change are **RegisteredOwner** and **RegisteredOrganization**, pointed to in Fig. 9.12.

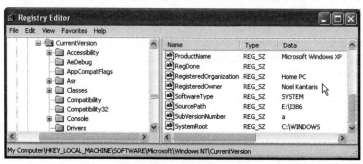

Fig. 9.12 The Registry Editor.

The **CurrentVersion** key, we are interested here, is to be found in the **Windows NT** branch, although you will find that there is a similarly named key in the **Windows** branch. Both branches are used by Windows XP, with the **Windows NT** branch containing the more advanced settings.

To change a Registry value, double-click it which opens the Edit String dialogue box shown in Fig. 9.13.

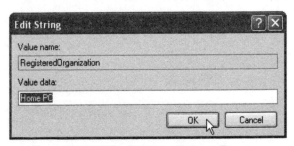

Fig. 9.13 The Edit String Dialogue Box.

You can type what you like in the **Value data** box to replace the current entry. Clicking the **OK** button enters the new value in the Registry. You can repeat this procedure to change the RegisteredOwner value to something else, then open the System Properties dialogue box again, as described earlier, to verify that your changes have taken place.

Note: Before closing the Registry Editor, left-click to highlight the **CurrentVersion** key. Next time you open the Registry Editor, this key will be expanded and displayed - the Editor remembers its previous position. In this way, if you need to make more changes to the values of this key, you will be assured that the correct key is selected automatically. Note also that the **Favorites** menu option, which works the same way as in the Internet Explorer, can be used to bookmark frequently accessed Registry keys.

2. The Auto-complete feature in Internet Explorer

The auto-complete feature was first introduced by Microsoft in their web browser Internet Explorer version 5. In the earlier versions, it was limited to the auto-completion of web addresses that you type in the browser's address bar. The later versions of Internet Explorer included auto-complete support for various form elements including form filling, e-mail addresses and passwords, etc.

If enabled, auto-complete lists possible matches for the entries you have typed before in Web-based forms. It can be enabled or disabled by using the Internet Explorer's **Tools**, **Internet Options**, command to display the dialogue box shown in Fig. 9.14 with its Content tab selected.

Fig. 9.14 The Internet Options Dialogue box.

Clicking the **AutoComplete** button, displays the dialogue box shown in Fig. 9.15 on the next page, from which you can enable (turn ON) or disable (turn OFF) the auto-complete feature for web addresses, forms and user names and passwords on forms.

You can also clear previous auto-complete entries on forms and passwords by clicking the appropriate buttons on the AutoComplete Setting dialogue box. Individual auto-complete entries can only be deleted from the Registry as we shall see shortly.

Fig. 9.15 The Internet Options Dialogue box.

To delete Web address entries, click the General tab on the Internet Options dialogue box (Fig. 9.14) and click the **Clear History** button.

To illustrate how it works, first we cleared the Web address entries in the General tab of the Internet Options dialogue box, then we typed the letter k in the Explorer's address bar, as shown here. The Explorer immediately  offers the address of the Web site which also happens to be the chosen 'Home Page' for this PC. Had we removed the check mark from the **Web address** box of Fig. 9.15 nothing would have been displayed by AutoComplete.

To activate the in-line AutoComplete feature for Web addresses, use the Internet Explorer's menu command **Tools**, **Internet Options**, click the Advanced tab, and under **Browsing**, click the **Use inline AutoComplete** check box, and then click **OK**.

To delete individual entries from the auto-complete list, go to:

HKEY_CURRENT_USER\Software\Microsoft\Internet Explorer\TypedURLs

This opens the screen shown in Fig. 9.16 below.

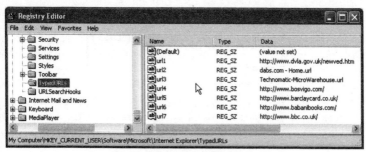

Fig. 9.16 The TypedURLs Key.

Obviously, the typed URLs will be different for your computer from the ones shown above. To remove an unwanted typed URL from the list, select it in the right pane of the Registry Editor, and press the **Delete** keyboard key. Needless to say, you have made a backup of the TypedURLs Registry key before you start deleting individual keys!

Below, we show a list of saved Registry keys and their relative size, starting with a full System State Backup of more than 368 MB, followed by two root keys of between 10 and 59 MB, down to a single key of 1 KB and its parent key of 44 KB. As you can see, you don't need large backup media to save a single key, or its parent key, so there is no excuse for not doing so!

System State Backup.bkf	368,620 KB	Windows Backup File
HKey_Local_Machine.reg	58,903 KB	Registration Entries
HKey_Current_User.reg	10,122 KB	Registration Entries
Internet Explorer.reg	44 KB	Registration Entries
TypedURLs.reg	1 KB	Registration Entries

Fig. 9.17 The Relative Size of Registry Keys.

Searching the Registry

The Registry is very large and very complex - it could contain more than 100,000 keys and values. Although the keys are organised into five major or root branches, the same keys can be found in more than one major branch.

For example, the branch HKEY_CURRENT_USER is a sub-branch (or symbolic link) of HKEY_USERS. Similarly, the branch HKEY_CLASSES_ROOT is a sub-branch (or symbolic link) of HKEY_LOCAL_MACHINE\SOFTWARE\Classes. Both of these are shown as root branches purely for convenience. Therefore, when you are looking for a certain key, you might find it in more than one of the five main Registry branches.

You can use the Registry Editor to help you find Registry keys, values, or data. Simply highlight a root key and use the **Edit**, **Find** command and in the displayed Find dialogue box, type the key to search for. It is here that you can specify where to look (**Keys**, **Values**, or **Data**) and what type of **Match** you require. In our example, shown in Fig. 9.18, we typed **URL** in the **Find what** box, selected **Keys** only and clicked the **Find Next** button. To continue the search for the same key, press the **F3** function key. Before long the key **TypedURLs** will be highlighted, as shown in Fig. 9.16.

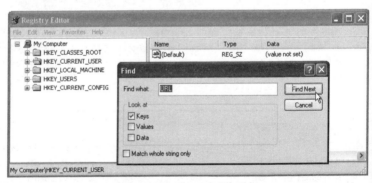

Fig. 9.18 Finding the URL Key.

The only way of finding your way around the Registry is by searching it and looking for keys that mean something to you.

Removing Startup Applications

If you are trying to remove a program and can not find it in the **StartUp** folder, by using the *start*, **All Programs** cascade menu command, then it might be launching itself from the HKEY_LOCAL_MACHINE registry key. To find it, go to:

    \SOFTWARE\Microsoft\Windows\CurrentVersion\Run

For one of our computers, the Registry screen, shown in Fig. 9.19, was displayed as follows.

Fig. 9.19 The
HKEY_LOCAL_MACHINE\SOFTWARE\Microsoft\Windows\CurrentVersion\
Run Screen.

On this particular computer the Hotkey application (the one that allows you to configure a button on your keyboard to load a preferred program when pressed), was loading and displaying on the Windows Task bar, thus taking unnecessary space. The offending entry in the Registry is pointed to in Fig. 9.19 and shown magnified below.

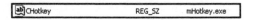

To remove it, either highlight the entry and press the **Delete** keyboard key, or double-click the entry and delete the value associated with that application. Whichever method we chose, it solved the problem at hand!

Three additional application entries in Fig. 9.19 were allowed at some time in the past to load on this computer, which now we would like to remove. These are displayed magnified below.

Share-to-Web Namespace Daemon	REG_SZ	C:\Program Files\Hewlett-Packard\HP Share-to-Web\hpgs2wnd.exe
SoundMan	REG_SZ	SOUNDMAN.EXE
SunJavaUpdateSched	REG_SZ	C:\Program Files\Java\j2re1.4.2_03\bin\jusched.exe

To remove these from our system, we simply highlighted each in turn and pressed the **Delete** keyboard button. To take effect, such removals require you to restart Windows.

With some applications you'll also have to check for entries in the

\SOFTWARE\Microsoft\Windows\CurrentVersion\RunOnce

branch of HKEY_LOCAL_MACHINE, as well as the entries in

\Software\Microsoft\Windows\CurrentVersion\Run

of the HKEY_CURRENT_USER branch.

Adding Startup Applications

To get a program to start automatically when starting Windows, open the Registry and go to:

\Software\Microsoft\Windows\CurrentVersion\Run

of the HKEY_CURRENT_USER branch and create a new string value by right-clicking empty space and using a descriptive name, and set its value to the program executable file. For example, to automatically start Notepad, add the entry shown in Fig. 9.20.

Fig. 9.20 Creating a New String Value.

Removing Uninstalled Programs

Occasionally you might find yourself in a situation where bits of programs have been left on your system and the **Add or Remove Programs** application in **Control Panel** is unable to uninstall them.

Although information on installed programs, as well as how to remove them, is kept in the Registry, sometimes an error on the program's uninstall configuration can result in bits of the program remaining in the system which might cause the system to become unstable.

To remove all traces of such programs, you need to edit the Registry. To start the process, open the Registry, and use the **Edit**, **Find** command and search for the **Uninstall** folder. Press the **F3** function key, until you reach the path:

HKEY_LOCAL_MACHINE\SOFTWARE\Microsoft\Windows\CurrentVersion\Uninstall

This sub-folder has entries which appear in the list of the **Add or Remove Programs** application in **Control Panel**. Each entry is displayed as a long name made up of letters and numbers, as shown in the left pane in Fig. 9.21 below.

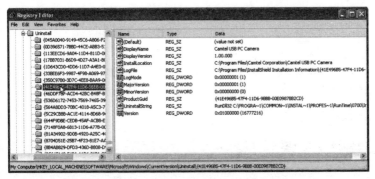

Fig. 9.21 The Contents of the Uninstall Folder.

Highlighting each entry on the left pane displays a list of program details on the right pane of the Editor. When you find the offending program, simply use the **Ctrl** key to highlight both the Display/Name and the UninstallString keys and press the **Delete** keyboard key.

Changing the Default Administrator Ownership

Sometimes, Windows XP might assign the ownership of some file system objects to the Administrator account, instead of to users who have Administrative rights. To change this, open the Registry and go to:

\SYSTEM\CurrentControlSet\Control\Lsa

of the HKEY_LOCAL_MACHINE branch and change the DWORD value of the NoDefaultAdminOwner key from 1 to 0, as shown in Fig. 9.22.

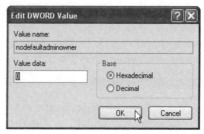

Fig. 9.22 Changing the DWORD of the NoDefaultAdminOwner Key.

Finally, exit the registry, and restart Windows for the change to take effect.

Starting a Program as an Administrator

If you want to set up a workstation or member server, then you must use the Administrator account, before creating an account for yourself. The Administrator account is a member of the Administrators group on the workstation or member server.

The Administrator account is the only account that cannot be deleted, disabled, or removed from the Administrators local group. Because of this, you can never lock yourself out of the computer by deleting or disabling all the administrative accounts. This feature makes the Administrator account different from all other members of the Administrators local group.

To start a program as an Administrator, do the following:

- In Windows Explorer, click the program executable file that you want to open.

- Press the **Shift** key and hold it down, then right-click the program icon, and then select the **Run as** command from the drop-down quick menu.

- In the displayed dialogue box, shown in Fig. 9.23, click **The following user** radio button to log on using the Administrator account.

Fig. 9.23 The Run As Dialogue Box.

Use this procedure if you want to perform administrative tasks when you are logged on as a member of another group, such as Users or Power Users.

Note: It is possible that you have been running your computer from an account under your own name which has administrative rights, and by now you have forgotten what you typed in as the Administrator password when you first used Setup to install Windows XP. If that is the case, not only you will be unable to carry on with the above procedure, but worse still, you will not be able to log onto the Recovery Console, as discussed in Chapter 10.

However, don't despair, there are programs out there that can help you find the forgotten password! Try searching the Internet for 'forgotten password'.

We used, and recommend, the Advanced Windows Recovery Password program from www.elcomsoft.com. There is a free, although restricted version (you can only find passwords up to three letters), but with excellent help files. The full version of the program can be activated once you have paid a modest fee for it, and it can deal with any length of forgotten passwords, not only within Windows XP, but also within other major Windows applications. Good luck!

10

Windows Recovery

Some of the information at the beginning of this Chapter is taken from the Windows Help files which you will not be able to access if Windows will not start. So being able to read this information on paper might be of help to you.

Startup Options

If Windows will not start for some reason, then turn off your computer and then back on again. As soon as any information starts being displayed on the screen, press the **F8** key. This displays the screen in Fig. 10.1 below.

```
Please select the operating system to start:

    Microsoft Windows XP Professional

Use the up and down arrow keys to move the highlight to your choice.
Press ENTER to choose.




For troubleshooting and advanced startup options for Windows, press F8.
```

Fig. 10.1 The First Startup Screen.

On this first screen you have two options; press **Enter** to start Microsoft Windows, or press **F8** again to access the advanced startup options. Pressing **F8**, displays the contents of Fig. 10.2 on the screen.

```
Windows Advanced Options Menu
Please select an option:

    Safe Mode
    Safe Mode with Networking
    Safe Mode with Command Prompt

    Enable Boot Logging
    Enable VGA Mode
    Last Known Good Configuration (your most recent settings that worked)
    Directory Services Restore Mode (Windows domain controllers only)
    Debugging Mode

    Start Windows Normally
    Reboot
    Return to OS Choices Menu

Use the up and down arrow keys to move the highlight to your choice.
```

Fig. 10.2 The Advanced Startup Options.

The various startup options allow the following capabilities:

Safe Mode

If your computer will not start, you might be able to start it in safe mode. In safe mode, Windows uses default settings (VGA monitor, Microsoft mouse driver (except serial mice), monitor, keyboard, mass storage, base video, and default system services, but no network connections.

This starting mode is used if your computer will not start after you install new software, which can be removed after starting your computer successfully in this mode. If a symptom does not reappear when you start in safe mode, you can eliminate the default settings and minimum device drivers as possible causes of the computer's inability to start.

If your computer does not start successfully using safe mode, you might need to use the Recovery Console feature to repair your system. This method will be discussed shortly.

Safe mode with Networking - Starts using only basic files and drivers, and network connections.

Safe mode with Command Prompt - Starts using only basic files and drivers. After logging on, the command prompt is displayed instead of the Windows graphical interface.

Enable Boot Logging - Starts while logging all the drivers and services that were loaded (or not loaded) by the system to a file. This file is called ntbtlog.txt and it is located in the %windir% directory. Safe Mode, Safe Mode with Networking, and Safe Mode with Command Prompt add to the boot log a list of all the drivers and services that are loaded. The boot log is useful in determining the exact cause of system startup problems.

Enable VGA Mode - Starts using the basic VGA driver. This mode is useful when you have installed a new driver for your video card that is causing Windows not to start properly. The basic video driver is always used when you start in Safe Mode (either Safe Mode, Safe Mode with Networking, or Safe Mode with Command Prompt).

Last Known Good Configuration

Starts using the Registry information and drivers that Windows saved at the last shutdown. Any changes made since the last successful startup will be lost. Use Last Known Good Configuration only in cases of incorrect configuration. It does not solve problems caused by corrupted or missing drivers or files.

Directory Service Restore Mode - This is for the server operating systems and is only used in restoring the SYSVOL directory and the Active Directory directory service on a domain controller.

Debugging Mode - Starts while sending debug information through a serial cable to another computer.

If you are using, or have used, Remote Installation Services to install Windows on your computer, you might see additional options related to restoring or recovering your system using Remote Install Services.

Using the Recovery Console

If Safe mode and other startup options do not work, you can consider using the Recovery Console. This method is recommended only if you are an advanced user who can use basic commands to identify and locate problem drivers and files. In addition, you must be an administrator and your Windows Setup disc must be current, that is, if you have updated your system to Windows Service Pack 1 or 2, then your Windows Setup CD must also contain this update, otherwise Windows will refuse to load an earlier version.

Using the Recovery Console, you can enable and disable services, format drives, read and write data on a local drive (including drives formatted to use NTFS), and perform many other administrative tasks. The Recovery Console is particularly useful if you need to repair your system by copying a file from a floppy disc or CD-ROM to your hard drive, or if you need to reconfigure a service that is preventing your computer from starting properly.

There are two ways to start the Recovery Console:

- If you are unable to start your computer, you can run the Recovery Console from your Setup CD.

- As an alternative, you can install the Recovery Console on your computer to make it available in case you are unable to restart Windows. You can then select the Recovery Console option from the list of available operating systems on startup.

To install the Recovery Console as a startup option, you must be running Windows, then insert the Setup CD into the CD-ROM drive, click *start* and select **Run**.

In the displayed Run dialogue box type the following where e: is the CD-ROM drive letter (yours might be different):

    e:\i386\winnt32.exe /cmdcons

then follow the instructions on the screen. These are as follows:

1) A dialogue box is displayed informing you that the Recovery Console requires 7 MB of disc space. You are asked whether to proceed or not.

2) You are asked to allow connection to the Internet so that the latest update to the Recovery Console can be obtained.

3) If you allow connection the necessary updates are downloaded, otherwise the existing files on the CD are used.

4) Files are copied onto your hard disc and a minute or so later, the following dialogue box is displayed.

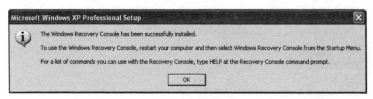

Microsoft Windows XP Professional Setup

The Windows Recovery Console has been successfully installed.

To use the Windows Recovery Console, restart your computer and then select Windows Recovery Console from the Startup Menu.

For a list of commands you can use with the Recovery Console, type HELP at the Recovery Console command prompt.

OK

Fig. 10.3 The Windows XP Setup Screen.

Now each time you start your computer, the following screen is displayed.

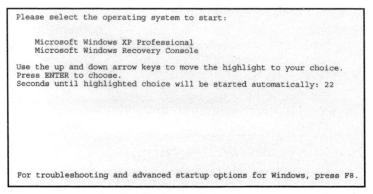

```
Please select the operating system to start:

    Microsoft Windows XP Professional
    Microsoft Windows Recovery Console

Use the up and down arrow keys to move the highlight to your choice.
Press ENTER to choose.
Seconds until highlighted choice will be started automatically: 22




For troubleshooting and advanced startup options for Windows, press F8.
```

Fig. 10.4 The Startup Options Screen.

Note: To run the Recovery Console, you must be logged on as an administrator or a member of the Administrators group in order to complete this procedure. If your computer is connected to a network, network policy settings may also prevent you from completing this procedure.

The console provides commands you can use to do simple operations such as changing to a different directory or viewing a directory, and more powerful operations such as fixing the boot sector. You can access Help for the commands in the Recovery Console by typing **help** at the Recovery Console command prompt once you are running the Recovery Console.

Recovery Console Commands

The following commands can be used with the Recovery Console:

Command	*Meaning*
Attrib	Changes the attributes of a file or directory.
Batch	Executes the commands specified in the text file.
Bootcfg	Boot file (boot.ini) configuration and recovery.
ChDir (Cd)	Displays the name of the current directory or changes the current directory.
Chkdsk	Checks a disc and displays a status report.
Cls	Clears the screen.
Copy	Copies a single file to another location.
Delete (Del)	Deletes one or more files.
Dir	Displays a list of files and sub-directories in a directory.

Disable	Disables a system service or a device driver.
Diskpart	Manages partitions on your hard drives.
Enable	Starts or enables a system service or a device driver.
Exit	Exits the Recovery Console and restarts the computer.
Expand	Extracts a file from a compressed file.
Fixboot	Writes a new partition boot sector onto the specified partition.
Fixmbr	Repairs the master boot record of the specified disc.
Format	Formats a disc.
Help	Displays a list of the commands you can use in the Recovery Console.
Listsvc	Lists the services and drivers available on the computer.
Logon	Logs on to a Windows installation.
Map	Displays the drive letter mappings.
Mkdir (Md)	Creates a directory.
More	Displays a text file.
Net Use	Connects a network share to a drive letter.
Rename (Ren)	Renames a single file.
Rmdir (Rd)	Deletes a directory.
Set	Displays and sets environment variables.
Systemroot	Sets the current directory to the systemroot directory of the system you are currently logged on to.
Type	Displays a text file.

Finally, you might be able to use the Recovery Console to access System Restore as follows: You start the Recovery Console, create a temporary folder, back up the existing registry files to a new location, delete the registry files at their existing location, and then copy the registry files from the repair folder to the System32\Config folder. When you have finished this procedure, a registry is created that you can use to start Windows XP. This registry was created and saved during the initial Windows XP installation, but changes that took place after the Setup program was finished are lost. The procedure is described in Microsoft's Knowledge Base Article 307545.

The article assumes that typical recovery methods have failed and access to the system is not available except by using Recovery Console. If an Automatic System Recovery (ASR) backup exists, it is the preferred method for recovery. Microsoft recommends that you use the ASR backup before you try the procedure described in the article.

Note: Microsoft warns you not to use the procedure described in the article if your computer has an OEM-installed operating system, as the system hive on OEM installations creates passwords and user accounts that did not exist previously. Using the procedure that is described in the article, might prevent you from logging back into the Recovery Console to restore the original Registry hives. If your PC uses an OEM installation get in touch with the manufacturer.

As you might be unable to refer to Microsoft's Knowledge Base should disaster strike, we suggest that you access Article 307545 while your computer is functioning normally, print it and put it in a safe place for future reference - it is far too complicated to summarise in this Chapter.

Finally, should you want to remove the Recovery Console from your hard disc, use the *start*, **Help and Support** menu option, and type Recovery Console in the **Search** box. In the displayed **Search Results** list, click the **Recovery Console overview** link, then click **Related topics** select the **Delete the Recovery Console** option, follow the displayed instructions and restart your computer.

Other Methods of Recovery

Below we discuss some alternative methods of recovery, one that you can download free from the Internet, and three that are classed as commercial, because you have to pay for them.

Bart Pre-installed Environment

Bart's Pre-installed Environment (BartPE) builder helps you create a bootable Windows CD-ROM or DVD from the original Windows XP (or Windows Server 2003) installation CD. Once this is burned onto a CD or DVD, it can be used to carry out many PC maintenance tasks.

To start the process, you need to connect to the Internet to Bart's Web site at www.nu2.nu/pebuilder and download the latest version of pebuilder, saving it on your hard disc. Once the download is complete, navigate to the location where you saved the download, and double-click the pebuilder.exe file.

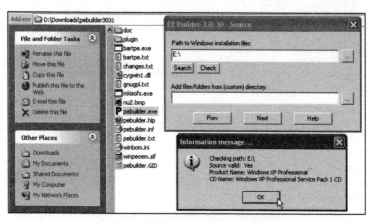

Fig. 10.5 The Downloaded BartPE files.

You will be asked to insert your Windows installation CD in the CD-ROM drive, after which the Information message box appears on your screen, as shown in Fig. 10.5 above. Clicking **OK** starts the process of building the required image.

On the next screen, you are asked to enable or disable various utilities and plug-ins, including network access, Nero Burning CD-ROM, McAfee's command-line virus scanner, and many more. In Fig. 10.6 we enabled the highlighted option.

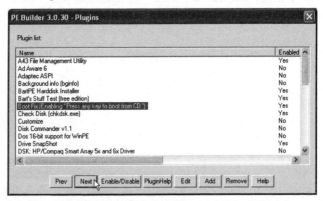

Fig. 10.6 Selecting Utilities and Plug-ins for the PE Builder.

Next, the program asks where to save the ISO image, as shown in Fig. 10.7, and proceeds to extract the core operating files from your Windows XP installation disc and uses them to create an ISO disc image.

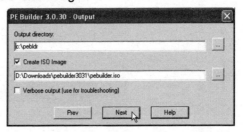

Fig. 10.7 Selecting the Drive to Save the ISO Image.

After some reading and writing activity the image is created, which you should burn on your CD-ROM as an image (not a file); this is important.

Not only can the BartPE see your primary hard drive, even if it has been converted into NTFS, but you have access to your network and CD-ROM drive once you have copied it onto your hard drive. You then need to be familiar with DOS commands.

Commercial Recovery Options

There are several commercial disaster recovery programs on the market; the most notable being Norton's Ghost, and Power Quest's Drive Image. Both of these can create a complete image of your hard drive which is by far the most secure method, with the advantage that it is independent of the state of your computer after disaster strikes. Such an image can be burned onto a CD or DVD using appropriate file compression.

On one of our computers we use Power Quest's Drive Image, making regular backups onto an external hard disc drive. The procedure is not dissimilar to the one used by Norton's Ghost. After installing the program, starting it displays the screen in Fig. 10.8 below.

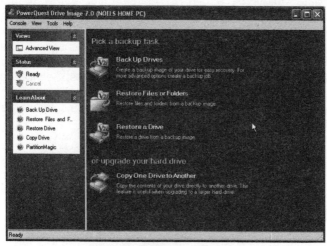

Fig. 10.8 Drive Image's Opening Screen.

From here, you can back up your drive, restore individual files or folders, restore an entire drive, or copy one drive to another. The program has very detailed help files which explain exactly what you can do and how to do it.

As we mentioned previously the program has the same capabilities, more or less, as those in Norton's Ghost. Which you use is a matter of preference.

Somewhere in between Bart's Pre-installed Environment and the above mentioned two programs lies a utility called VCOM Recovery Commander (www.guildsoft.co.uk). This program creates regular 'checkpoints' of your system, by saving the Registry, boot record, and other important files. The program can also create an ISO image file that you can burn on your CD-ROM which can then be used to provide access to the computer and its saved checkpoints.

Note: We strongly suggest that you investigate a drive imaging method of System Recovery. You might not believe that anything bad could happen to your computer, but given time, it will. For example, your hard disc might malfunction, or your computer might be stolen, to mention but a few of many possible and unforeseen disasters. With an image of your hard drive sitting somewhere safe, the problem could be overcome in less than 30 minutes. Without it you could spend weeks getting your programs and data back in order. Imagine having to first reinstall Windows, then reinstall the latest Service Pack and all the critical updates, then reinstall all your application programs, then configure all of them, before you could find and mount your precious data!

11

Windows VBScripts

The ability to write scripts is of paramount importance in computing. Scripts allow you to automate repetitive tasks and prior to Windows 98 this could only be achieved with the rather limited batch files under DOS.

With the release of Windows 98, Microsoft made available the Windows Script Host (WSH) which, at first, provided a way to automate Windows-based graphical applications using the two scripting languages VBScript and JScript. However, since the first release of WSH, third-party add-ons made this script host capable of running scripts written in other languages, such as Perl and Python, to mention but a few. You don't need the full scripting programs on your computer to run such scripts, as WSH has all the necessary libraries, etc., required to accomplish the task.

Today, the latest version of WSH can be used to create complex scripts to automate not only Windows-based graphical applications, such as running of XML encoded scripts natively within the operating system, but also network login, Registry access, and Desktop tasks. Since WSH was first provided to host VBScript and JScript, knowing something of the background of these two languages is a good starting point.

Early Windows Scripting Support

JScript
JScript is an interpreted, object-based scripting language. Although it has fewer capabilities than fully-fledged object-oriented languages like C++, JScript is more than sufficiently powerful for its intended purposes.

JScript, although distantly related to Java, is not a cut-down version of it or any other language. It is, however, limited in that you cannot write stand-alone applications in it, and it has no built-in support for reading from, or writing to, files.

Scripts written in JScript can run only in the presence of an interpreter or 'host', such as Active Server Pages (ASP), Internet Explorer, or Windows Script Host (WSH).

VBScript

Microsoft Visual Basic Scripting Edition (VBScript) brings active scripting to a wide variety of environments, including Web client scripting in Microsoft Internet Explorer and Web server scripting in Microsoft Internet Information Service.

If you already know Visual Basic or Visual Basic for Applications (VBA), VBScript will be very familiar. Although we can show you what VBScript can do in just a few pages, we cannot teach you how to become a programmer in the space available in this book. If you want to learn how to program in Visual Basic, may we suggest our book *Using Visual Basic* (BP498) also published by Bernard Babani (publishing) Ltd.

Scripts can be created in a text editor such as Notepad and saved as ANSI (text) format. If you use Word or Wordpad, save the script as a text file, not in their native format. In all cases, the file extension relates to the language the script was created in, for example, **.vbs** for VBScript.

Below, we demonstrate the creation and execution of a very simple script. First open Notepad and type the information shown in Fig. 11.1.

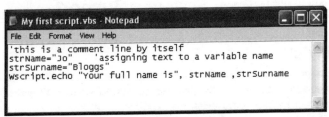

Fig. 11.1 A Very Simple Script.

As you can see, the first and second lines of the script includes a comment by preceding it by a single quote ('). Comment lines are used to remind you what you were thinking at the time of writing the script, and are essential particularly for larger scripts.

On the second and third lines of the script we assign a text to a variable. A variable is used to store information for use during the processing of the script - it can be text information such as a name, a number, a date, or a reference to an object. A variable name can be any combination of letters and numbers, but it cannot contain spaces.

It is usual to give variable names descriptive names, and prefix them with a few characters to identify the type of variable. In the table below, we give examples of variable name prefixes.

Prefix	Type	Example
str	String - any letters of numbers or characters that are available on a keyboard	strName
num	Number	numAge
int	Integer - whole number without decimals	intCount
dat	Date	datBirthDate
b	Boolean - with values of True (-1 or any positive number) or False (0)	bFlag
obj	Object	objEmail

Variables do not have to be declared explicitly in VBScript, unlike other languages, such as C++ where this is a must. However, it is a good idea to declare variables before using them for two reasons; clarity and debugging purposes. You declare a variable with the statement

```
dim variablename
```

It is also wise to force explicit declaration of variables by adding the satatement

```
Option Explicit
```

At the beginning of a script. This will cause VBScript to generate an error if a variable was misspelled due to a typo. If you made such a mistake and did not use the above option, VBScript will not catch the error - the script will simply not work.

Assignment of values to variables is achieved with the equals sign (=). For example,

```
Variablename = value
```

with different types of data being assigned in different ways. For example,

```
strSurname = "Bloggs"

intAge = 35

numWeight = 80.5

datBirthDate = #5/1/80#        interpretation depends
                               on system settings

intCount = intCount + 5        adds 5 to the value of
                               intCount

strFullName =  strName &" " & strSurname

StrNameAndWeight = strFullName & " is " &
                   numWeight & "Kgs in weight"
```

In the last example we assign a combination of various types of variables to one variable name.

Finally, in the fourth line of our example (Fig. 11.1) we used one of the supplied Windows XP programs (wscript.exe - more about this later) to echo the result on the screen. Having typed all four lines of the script into Notepad, as shown in Fig. 11.1, use the **File**, **Save As** command to save it with the extension **.vbs**, but as a text file, ANSI encoded, as shown in Fig. 11.2.

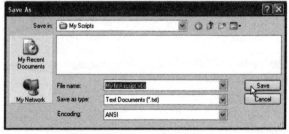

Fig. 11.2 Saving a Simple Script.

To edit a saved script, right-click it and choose **Edit** from the drop-down menu.

Windows XP comes with two programs that can run scripts; wscript.exe is used to run scripts from the Windows graphical environment, while cscript.exe is used to run scripts from the command line or from within batch files.

Fig. 11.3 The Properties Dialogue Box of a Simple Script.

To use wscript.exe to run scripts under Windows, locate the saved **.vbs** file, right-click it and select **Properties** from the drop-down menu. This opens the Properties dialogue box shown in Fig. 11.3. From here you can change the **Open with** option, if need be, for files with the **.vbs** extension. You can also choose whether the script should time out, what the time out should be, and whether the script logo should be displayed when the script is run.

To execute our simple script, double-click its name which displays the message shown here to the left.

You can also run a script by using the *start*, **Run** command, browsing to the location of the saved script, as shown in Fig. 11.4.

Fig. 11.4 Running a Script from the Run Box.

To run a script from the **Command Prompt**, you must first rename the script filename by replacing all spaces with underscores, then (if necessary) change the drive where the script is to be found, change the directory so that it points to the location of the file, and type **wscript** followed by the filename, as shown below.

```
D:\My Documents\My Scripts>wscript My_first_script.vbs
```

Security and the Windows Script Host

Apart from running scripts, the Windows Script Host creates an environment for hosting scripts that might arrive at your computer, by making objects and services available for such a script and providing a set of guidelines within which the script is executed. Among other things, WSH manages security and invokes the appropriate script engine.

Trusting Scripts

When a script or a macro is about to be executed on your PC, whether it has arrived from the Internet or is included in a resident application, WSH examines the

HKEY_CURRENT_USER\Software\Microsoft\Windows Script Host\Settings

registry key and looks for the TrustPolicy DWORD. If that DWORD is not under HKEY_CURRENT_USER, then it looks for it under the HKEY_LOCAL_MACHINE, as shown below in Fig. 11.5. WSH then determines if it should verify trust before running the code.

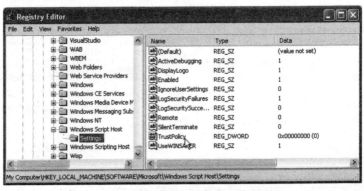

Fig. 11.5 The TrustPolicy Registry Key.

In the registry, the trust policy is set to one of three values: 0, 1, or 2. A value of 0 means run trusted scripts. A value of 1 means prompt the user if asked to run an untrustworthy script. Finally, a value of 2 means do not prompt the user and do not run untrustworthy scripts.

Fig. 11.6 Editing a DWORD Value.

To change the value of the policy key, double-click the TrustPolicy entry on the right pane of the Registry Editor which opens the screen in Fig. 11.6. Perhaps the best value to give to this DWORD is 2, but it is up to you.

Downloading the Latest WSH Version

To download the latest Windows Script Host version 5.1, go to

```
http://msdn.microsoft.com/library
```

and search for 'scripts'. In the displayed Web page, click the 'Windows Script Developer Center' link, followed by the 'Microsoft Windows Script 5.6 Download' link.

Examples Using the Windows Script Host

As we have seen, scripts are built by typing commands, one on each line. Commands are used to either set a specific property of an object to some value, or to carry out some action. Much of VBScript involves referencing objects and setting properties. Most scripts will require the following line:

```
Set wshShell = wscript.CreateObject("wscript.Shell")
```

which creates the wshShell object. The various properties and methods of this object are used to accomplish many tasks in VBScript, such as displaying message boxes and retrieving system information. The code in Fig. 11.7, displayed on the next page, shows two such examples. In Chapter 11 we include a list of Functions, Statements, Operators, Objects, and Constants, which should be referred to in conjunction with the examples presented here.

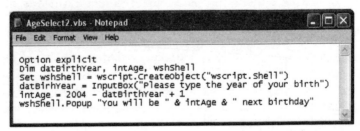

```
AgeSelect1.vbs - Notepad
File  Edit  Format  View  Help

Set wshShell = wscript.CreateObject("wscript.Shell")
datBirthYear = InputBox("Please type the year of your birth")
intAge = 2004 - datBirthYear + 1
wshShell.Popup "You will be " & intAge & " next birthday"
```

Fig. 11.7 Setting Properties and Referencing Objects Example.

In the first line we create a wshShell object to be used in the Popup statement later in the script. The second line asks the user to type their age in an Input box, and then assigns the typed value into the variable datBirthYear. The third line then creates a new variable, intAge, and subtracts datBirthYear from the current year and adds 1 to the result. Do note that we have not included any error checking; if the user does not enter a number, this statement will cause a 'type mismatch' error. The fourth line then concatenates a text string to the variable intAge, and displays the result in a message box. We could have used the wscript.echo statement we used in our first example.

Using this simple syntax, you can create more useful scripts that launch and control applications, make changes to the Registry, and communicate with the network. But before we go any further, let us edit the AgeSelect1.vbs script to include variable declaration, and the explicit option we discussed earlier. In Fig. 11.8 below, we have added two lines at the beginning of the script and edited the beginning of line 4, so that instead of datBirthYear it now reads datBirhYear.

```
AgeSelect2.vbs - Notepad
File  Edit  Format  View  Help

Option explicit
Dim datBirthYear, intAge, wshShell
Set wshShell = wscript.CreateObject("wscript.Shell")
datBirhYear = InputBox("Please type the year of your birth")
intAge = 2004 - datBirthYear + 1
wshShell.Popup "You will be " & intAge & " next birthday"
```

Fig. 11.8 Setting Properties and Referencing Objects Example.

Fig. 11.9 Error Message.

Save the resulting script as AgeSelect2.vbs, and run it. An error message is displayed, as shown here in Fig. 11.9, telling you precisely why and where the error has occurred.

Next, correct the spelling of the variable name that caused the error, and re-save the script under the same name. As you can see, it is worth adding the extra statements to trap typos.

Using Functions in Scripts

In the example below (Fig. 11.10) we substituted the current year (2004) in the code of line 5 of our previous example (script AgeSelect2.vbs) with two functions.

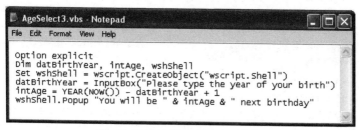

```
Option explicit
Dim datBirthYear, intAge, wshShell
Set wshShell = wscript.CreateObject("wscript.shell")
datBirthYear = InputBox("Please type the year of your birth")
intAge = YEAR(NOW()) - datBirthYear + 1
wshShell.Popup "You will be " & intAge & " next birthday"
```

Fig. 11.10 Using Functions in a Script.

These two functions return the following values:

The Now() function returns the current date and time of your computer's system date and time. The function needs no arguments between the parentheses, and

the Year() function is used to determine the year from the supplied date variable or formatted string which should be supplied within the parentheses. In this case the required argument is supplied by the returned value of the NOW() function.

Therefore, the result of using these two functions in the manner indicated above, is to return a number which depends on the year you run the script. If you run the script in 2004, the returned number will be 2004, if you run it in 2005, the return number will be 2005, etc. Save the resultant script as AgeSelect3.vbs.

Please Note: In Chapter 12, we list all the functions you can use in Windows VBScript, with a description of what each function does. Obviously we can not give examples of each of these functions in the space allotted, but you can find examples of usage on the Internet. Use Google as your search engine (www.google.com) and type "wsh VBScript Functions" (without the quotes) as the search criteria. Good luck!

Error Detection in Scripts

Returning to our example AgeSelect3.vbs (Fig. 11.10), if when asked to enter the year of your birth you were simply to press the **Enter** key instead, the script would produce a mismatch error as shown in Fig. 11.11.

Fig. 11.11 Error Message.

To overcome such an error, include line 5 in the script, as shown in Fig. 11.12 below.

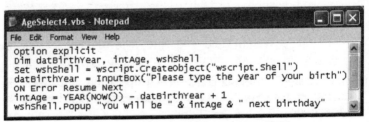

```
option explicit
Dim datBirthYear, intAge, wshShell
set wshShell = wscript.CreateObject("wscript.Shell")
datBirthYear = InputBox("Please type the year of your birth")
ON Error Resume Next
intAge = YEAR(NOW()) - datBirthYear + 1
wshShell.Popup "You will be " & intAge & " next birthday"
```

Fig. 11.12 Using an Error Statement in a Script.

The statement

```
On Error Resume Next
```

provides a limited amount of error handling by preventing program flow interruption from a runtime error. When an error occurs, the line of code containing the error is simply skipped over and the program continues running. Therefore the placement of the On Error statement is crucial, as when the error occurs it is just ignored, and the error message is not displayed.

Next, we have modified the script AgeSelect4.vbs to include a more complex error routine, as shown in Fig. 11.13 below. This routine incorporates a few more functions as well as the **If ... Then ... Else ... End If** statement. The **If** part of the **If ... Else** statement conditionally executes groups of statements only when a single test condition is **True**, while the **Else ... End If** part of the statement conditionally executes groups of statements only when the test **If** condition is **False**.

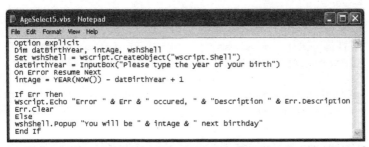

Fig. 11.13 Using The If Then Else End If Statement in an Error Routine.

What happens here is that the occurrence of an error, if it takes place, is reported within the **If ... Else** part of the statement without halting the execution of the script, while an answer is displayed, if no error occurs, within the **Else ... End If** part of the statement.

Here is an example of a more complex script. Let us say you want to enter your date of birth and have the script calculate and print your age in years, months and days. The script in Fig. 11.14 shown on the next page will do just that.

AgeSelect6.vbs - Notepad

```
  Option explicit
  Dim datBirthDate, intYears, intMonths, intDays, wshShell
  Set wshShell = wscript.CreateObject("wscript.Shell")
 Do
  datBirthDate = InputBox("Please type the date of your birth in the
form dd/mm/yyyy")
  On Error Resume Next
  intYears = YEAR(NOW()) - YEAR(datBirthDate)
  intMonths = ABS(MONTH(NOW()) - MONTH(datBirthDate))
  intDays = ABS(DAY(NOW()) - DAY(datBirthDate))
  If Err Then
  Wscript.Echo "Please enter a valid date"
  Err.Clear
  Elseif intYears > 110 Then Wscript.Echo intYears & " Years? Please
enter a valid date"
  Elseif DateValue(datBirthDate) = 0 Then Exit Do
  Else
  wshShell.Popup "You are " & intYears & " Years, "& intMonths & "
Months and " & intDays & " Days old"
  Exit Do
  End If
 Loop
```

Fig. 11.14 A Script to Calculate Exact Age.

Please note than the code in lines 6, 15, and 19 (the ones that start at the far left of the screen dump above), are part of lines 5, 14, and 18, respectively, and should be entered in Notepad as a continuation of the latter.

This script makes use of several different statements and functions which we shall try to explain below. We start by declaring 5 variables, **datBirthDate** to hold the date of birth, **intYears**, **intMonths**, and **intDays** to hold the whole number of years, months, and days from the date of birth to the present date.

Next, the script sets a **Do ... Loop** statement which repeats all statements between the **Do** and the **Loop** lines, until some specific criteria are met. These are:

(a) if the user has clicked the ☒ button on the opening **Inbox**, and

(b) if the correct input format for the date of birth was entered in the **Inbox** and an answer was displayed.

When either of the above criteria is met, the **Do ... Loop** statement is halted with the statement **Exit Do**.

Next, we introduce the **If ... Elseif ... Else ... End If** statement. From its structure you can see how you can have several **Elseif** statements embedded within the **If** and **Else** lines.

As you can see, VBScripts resemble programs written in Visual Basic, so if you have any programming experience, writing VBScripts should be quite easy. As we have also seen, VBScript is an interpreted language, which means that you do not need to compile your scripts as you would with a program written in C or C++. Your scripts are directly interpreted, line-by-line, when they are executed in the user's Windows Script Host or Internet Explorer browser.

Web Page Scripts

Below we show where to insert a VBScript in a Web page. The **MsgBox** function (which is our entire script here) is placed between the <SCRIPT> tags, with comment tags (<!-- and -->) on either side of it.

```
<HTML>
<HEAD>
<TITLE>My First IE VBScript</TITLE>
<SCRIPT LANGUAGE="VBScript">
<!--
MsgBox "Hello World!"
-->
</SCRIPT>
</HEAD>
</HTML>
```

As Internet Explorer is the only browser that supports VBScripts, the inclusion of the comment tags avoids having the code of VBScripts being displayed as text on browsers that do not support it - the comment tags cause the code of such scripts to appear as a comment, and is ignored.

Save the above script code under the filename **Web script1.htm** (note the extension), then locate it and double-click it. A message box is displayed, as shown here, in Internet Explorer.

The VBScript in Fig. 11.15 is slightly more complicated than our previous example, but as we explain it, you will see that it is quite easy to understand.

```
Web script2.htm - Notepad
File Edit Format View Help
<HTML>
<HEAD>
<TITLE>My second Web page VBScript</TITLE>
<BODY>
<H2>The Second Web VBScript</H2>
<P> Type in 3 numbers in the fields below and click the "Calculate Average" button
</P>
<FORM NAME="frmExample">
<TABLE>
    <TR>
        <TD><B>Number 1:</B></TD>
        <TD><INPUT TYPE="Text" NAME="strNumber1" SIZE=5></TD>
    </TR>
    <TR>
        <TD><B>Number 2:</B></TD>
        <TD><INPUT TYPE="Text" NAME="strNumber2" SIZE=5></TD>
    </TR>
    <TR>
        <TD><B>Number 3:</B></TD>
        <TD><INPUT TYPE="Text" NAME="strNumber3" SIZE=5></TD>
    </TR>
</TABLE>
    <BR>
    <INPUT TYPE="Button" NAME="cmdCalculate" VALUE="Calculate Average">
</FORM>
</BODY>
<SCRIPT LANGUAGE="VBScript">
<!--
Option Explicit
Sub cmdCalculate_OnClick
    Dim strNumber1, strNumber2, strNumber3, numAmount1, numAmount2, numAmount3,
numAverage, strMessage
 ' Perform average calculations
    numAmount1 = Document.frmExample.strNumber1.Value
    numAmount2 = Document.frmExample.strNumber2.Value
    numAmount3 = Document.frmExample.strNumber3.Value
    numAverage = numAmount1/3.0 + numAmount2/3.0 + numAmount3/3.0
 ' Display the results
    strMessage = "Average of 3 numbers is: " & numAverage
    MsgBox strMessage,, "Average"
End Sub
-->
</SCRIPT>
</HEAD>
```

Fig. 11.15 A Script to Calculate the Average of Three Numbers.

Type the above code into Notepad and save it under the fileneme **Web script2.htm**. Next, locate it and double-click it to display what is shown here in Fig. 11.16. If this display does

not appear for you in your Internet Explorer, then check each line of the code very carefully to identify any mistakes.

Fig. 11.16 Running the Second Web VBScript.

In this example, we create an HTML document which contains a script that will retrieve data from the Web page, shown in Fig. 11.16, perform several calculations and output a result.

In the HTML code of our example, after giving our Web page a title, a heading, and instructions on what to type in the Web form, we demonstrate how values are taken from a form and used within a script. The three fields on the form were named **strNumber1**, **strNumber2**, and **strNumber3** in their HTML <INPUT> tags, with the form being named **frmExample**. So, here we are referencing the web document, then the form, then the input field.

After the starting <SCRIPT> tag and the HTML comment tag for the benefit of non-Internet Explorer browsers, we include the Option Explicit statement which forces us to declare all our variables. We then create the sub procedure, called (cmdCalculate_OnClick), for the click event of the 'Calculate Average' screen button, followed by the declaration of eight variables which are procedure-level declarations since they are declared within a procedure.

Next, and within the comments 'Perform average Calculations' and 'Display the Results', we first convert the input entered on the three fields of the form into values and store them into variables **numAmout1**, **numAmout2**, and **numAmount3**. The last line of calculation works out the value of the average of the three numbers and stores it in variable **numAverage**.

As we have mentioned before, anything after an apostrophe is a comment and is ignored when the script is executed. Comments can appear on a line by themselves or at the end of a line of script. The / sign in the calculation line indicates division, while the + sign indicates addition. Other commonly used VBScript operands are: * for multiplication, and - for subtraction.

Finally, the ampersand character (&) in the statement following the 'Display the results' comment, is used to concatenate two strings, and the result of our calculation is displayed using the **MsgBox** function.

Finally, the example in Fig. 11.17 can give you the current date in a rather full form. We use this example to demonstrate how you can use arrays. Remember that the 1st element of an array, say, 'months' is months(0) and, therefore, the 9th element is months(8).

```
Web script3.htm - Notepad
File  Edit  Format  View  Help
<HTML>
<HEAD>
<TITLE>My third web page Script</TITLE>
<BODY>
<H2>The third web Script</H2>
<SCRIPT LANGUAGE="VBScript">
<!--
 option Explicit
 Dim strTodaysDate, strordinal, numDay, numMonth, numYear, months(11)
  numDay = Day((NOW))
  numMonth = Month(NOW())
  numYear = Year(NOW())
    months(0) = "January"
    months(1) = "February"
    months(2) = "March"
    months(3) = "April"
    months(4) = "May"
    months(5) = "June"
    months(6) = "July"
    months(7) = "August"
    months(8) = "September"
    months(9) = "October"
    months(10) = "November"
    months(11) = "December"
    strordinal = "th "
    If numDay = 3 Then
      strordinal = "rd "
    Elseif numDay = 23 Then
      strordinal = "rd "
    Elseif numDay = 2 Then
      strordinal = "nd "
    Elseif numDay = 22 Then
      strordinal = "nd "
    Elseif numDay = 1 Then
      strordinal = "st "
    Elseif numDay = 21 Then
      strordinal = "st "
    Elseif numDay = 31 Then
      strordinal = "st "
    End If
   strTodaysDate = numDay & " "& strordinal & " " & months(numMonth-1) & ", " & numYear
MsgBox strTodaysDate,, "Today's Date:"
-->
</SCRIPT>
</HEAD>
</HTML>
```

Fig. 11.17 A Script to Display the Current Date.

Apart from the use of arrays, the above program shows you how to manipulate dates, and how to structure an **If ... Elseif ... End If** statement. We suggest you try to work out how this program achieves its goal.

In this chapter, we have given you a little taste of VBScripts. However, to cover even the most commonly used Function, Statements, Operators, Constants, and Objects, we would need to write a dedicated book on these items alone. One never knows, if it keeps raining as it does while we are writing this, we might be motivated enough to undertake such a task!

12

VBScript Commands

Functions

Array Functions

Array(arglist)
: Returns a variant containing an array

Filter(inputStrings, value)
: Returns a zero-based array that contains a subset of a string array based on a filter criteria

IsArray(varname)
: Returns a Boolean value that indicates whether a specified variable is an array

Join(list)
: Returns a string that consists of a number of sub-strings in an array

LBound(arrayname)
: Returns the smallest subscript for the indicated dimension of an array

Split(expression)
: Returns a zero-based, one-dimensional array that contains a specified number of sub-strings

UBound(arrayname)
: Returns the largest subscript for the indicated dimension of an array

Conversion Functions

Asc(string)

Converts the first letter in a string to ANSI code

CBool(expression)

Converts an expression to a variant of subtype Boolean

CByte(expression)

Converts an expression to a variant of subtype Byte

CCur(expression)

Converts an expression to a variant of subtype Currency

CDate(date)

Converts a valid date and time expression to the variant of subtype Date

CDbl(expression)

Converts an expression to a variant of subtype Double

Chr(chrcode)

Converts the specified ANSI code to a character

CInt(expression)

Converts an expression to a variant of subtype Integer

CLng(expression)

Converts an expression to a variant of subtype Long

CSng(expression)

Converts an expression to a variant of subtype Single

CStr(expression)

Converts an expression to a variant of subtype String

Date/Time Functions

CDate(date)	Converts a valid date and time expression to the variant of subtype Date
Date()	Returns the current system date
DateAdd(interval, number, date)	Returns a date to which a specified time interval has been added
DateDiff(interval, date1, date2)	Returns the number of intervals between two dates
DatePart(interval, date)	Returns the specified part of a given date
DateSerial(year, month, day)	Returns the date for a specified year, month, and day
DateValue(date)	Returns a date
Day(date)	Returns a number that represents the day of the month (between 1 and 31, inclusive)
FormatDateTime(date)	Returns an expression formatted as a date or time
Hour(time)	Returns a number that represents the hour of the day (between 0 and 23, inclusive)
IsDate(expression)	Returns a Boolean value that indicates if the evaluated expression can be converted to a date

Minute(time)	Returns a number that represents the minute of the hour (between 0 and 59, inclusive)
Month(date)	Returns a number that represents the month of the year (between 1 and 12, inclusive)
MonthName(month)	Returns the name of a specified month
Now()	Returns the current system date and time
Second(time)	Returns a number that represents the second of the minute (between 0 and 59)
Time()	Returns the current system time
Timer()	Returns the number of seconds since 12:00 am
TimeSerial(hour, minute, second)	Returns the time for a specific hour, minute, and second
TimeValue(time)	Returns a time
Weekday(date)	Returns a number that represents the day of the week (between 1 and 7, inclusive)
WeekdayName(weekday)	Returns the weekday name of a specified day of the week
Year(date)	Returns a number that represents the year

Format Functions

FormatCurrency(expression)	Returns an expression formatted as a currency value
FormatDateTime(date)	Returns an expression formatted as a date or time
FormatNumber(expression)	Returns an expression formatted as a number
FormatPercent(expression)	Returns an expression formatted as a percentage

Math Functions

Abs(number)	Returns the absolute value of a specified number
Atn(number)	Returns the arctangent of a specified number
Cos(number)	Returns the cosine of a specified number (angle)
Exp(number)	Returns e raised to a power
Hex(number)	Returns the hexadecimal value of a specified number
Int(number)	Returns the integer part of a specified number
Fix(number)	Returns the integer part of a specified number
Log(number)	Returns the natural logarithm of a specified number

Oct(number)	Returns the octal value of a specified number
Rnd(number)	Returns a random number less than 1 but greater or equal to 0
Sgn(number)	Returns an integer that indicates the sign of a specified number
Sin(number)	Returns the sine of a specified number (angle)
Sqr(number)	Returns the square root of a specified number
Tan(number)	Returns the tangent of a specified number (angle)

String Functions

InStr(string1, string2)	Returns the position of the first occurrence of one string within another. The search begins at the first character of the string
InStrRev(string1, string2)	Returns the position of the first occurrence of one string within another. The search begins at the last character of the string
LCase(string)	Converts a specified string to lowercase
Left(string, length)	Returns a specified number of characters from the left side of a string

Len(string | varname)	Returns the number of characters in a string or number of bytes required to store a variable
LTrim(string)	Removes spaces on the left side of a string
RTrim(string)	Removes spaces on the right side of a string
Trim(string)	Removes spaces on both the left and the right side of a string
Mid(string, start)	Returns a specified number of characters from a string
Replace(expression, find, replacewith	Replaces a specified part of a string with another string a specified number of times
Right(string, length)	Returns a specified number of characters from the right side of a string
Space(number)	Returns a string that consists of a given number of spaces
StrComp(string1, string2)	Compares two strings and returns a value that represents the result of the comparison
String(number, character)	Returns a string that contains a repeating character of a specified length
StrReverse(string)	Reverses a string
UCase(string)	Converts a string to uppercase

Other Functions

CreateObject(server1.type)	Creates an object called server1 of a specified type
Eval(expression)	Evaluates an expression and returns the result
GetLocale()	Returns the current locale ID
GetObject([pathname])	Returns a reference to an automation object from a file
GetRef(procname)	Allows you to connect a VBScript procedure to a DHTML event on your pages
InputBox(prompt)	Displays a dialogue box, where the user can write some input and/or click on a button, and returns the contents
IsEmpty(expression)	Returns a Boolean value that indicates whether a specified variable has been initialized
IsNull(expression)	Returns a Boolean value that indicates whether a specified expression contains no valid data (Null)
IsNumeric(expression)	Returns a Boolean value that indicates whether a specified expression can be evaluated as a number
IsObject(expression)	Returns a Boolean value that indicates whether the specified expression is an automation object

LoadPicture(picturename)	Returns a picture object, but only on 32-bit platforms
MsgBox(prompt)	Displays a message box, waits for you to click a button, and returns a value that indicates which button was clicked
RGB(red, green, blue)	Returns a number that represents an RGB colour value
Round(expression)	Rounds a number
ScriptEngine	Returns the scripting language in use
ScriptEngineBuildVersion	Returns the build version number of the scripting engine in use
ScriptEngineMajorVersion( )	Returns the major version number of the scripting engine in use
ScriptEngineMinorVersion( )	Returns the minor version number of the scripting engine in use
SetLocale(lcid)	Sets the locale ID and returns the previous locale ID
TypeName(varname)	Returns the subtype of a specified variable
VarType(varname)	Returns a value that indicates the subtype of a specified variable

Statements

Call(arg1, arg2, ...)	Used to call a function or subroutine and pass one or more arguments to them
Class ... End Class	Used to create a class statement block
Const	Allows the declaration of constants
Dim	Allows the explicit declaration of one or more variables
Do Until ... Loop	Repeats a block of code until a condition becomes true
Do While ... Loop	Repeats a block of code while a condition is satisfied
Erase	Used to empty arrays
Execute(Sring)	Interprets a single string as a statement or sequence of statements and executes them
Exit	Allows exit from inside a block of code as a conditional statement
For ... Next	Repeats a block of code a number of specified times
For Each ... Next	For Each condition statement it repeats a block of code for each element of an array or a collection of data

Function Name(arg1, arg2) ... End Function	Passes values to the function through the argument list, but returns a single value (in the Name of the function) back from where it was called
If ... Then	It executes groups of statements only when a single test condition is True
On Error Resume Next	Gives a limited amount of error handling by preventing program interruption by errors
On Error GoTo 0	Disables error handling
Option Explicit	Forces the explicit declaration of all variables
Private	Used to declare a new variable or array
Property Get ... End Property	Allows you to perform a procedure that will return the value of the property
Property Let ... End Property	Allows you to perform a procedure that assigns the value of a property
Property Set ... End Property	Allows you to perform a procedure that sets a reference to an object
Public	Used to declare a new public variable or array
Randomize	Gives the Rnd function a new seed value for generating random numbers

ReDim	Allows you to re-size a dynamic array, thus also re-sizing the memory allocated to it
Rem or '	Allows the insertion of comments
Select Case	It selectively executes different groups of code
Set	Assigns the object reference to a variable or property
Sub Name(arg1, arg2, ...)	Creates a Name(d) subroutine and allows you to pass values to it, and back, via the argument list
While ... WEnd	Conditionally repeats a block of code as long as the test condition remains True
With ... End With	Allows the execution of code on the named object

Operators

And	Used to perform a logical conjunction on two expressions
Eqv	Used to perform a logical comparison on two expressions
Imp	Used to perform a logical implication on two expressions
Is	Used to determine if two variables refer to the same object
Mod	Used to divide two numbers and return the remainder
Not	Used to perform a logical negation on two expressions
Or	Used to perform a logical disjunction on two expressions
Xor	Used to perform a logical exclusion on two expressions
=	Assigns a value to a variable
<	Determines if the first expression is less than the second

>	Determines if the first expression is greater than the second
<=	Determines if the first expression is less than or equal to the second
>=	Determines if the first expression is greater than or equal to the second
<>	Determines if the first expression is not equal to the second
*	Used to multiply numbers or contents of variables
/	Used to divide numbers or contents of variable - returns a floating point number
\	Used to divide numbers or contents of variable - returns an integer number
*	Used to multiply numbers or contents of variables
+	Used to add numbers or contents of variables
&	Used to concatenate strings
-	Used to subtract numbers or contents of variables
^	Used to raise a number or a variable to a power

Objects

Class ... End Class	Allows the creation of objects on which operations can be performed
Dictionary	Used to store name/value pairs in an array
Drive	Provides access to various properties of the local or remote disc drives
Drive Collection	Collection of all drives available on the system
Err	Holds information about the last runtime error that occurred
File	Allows access and handling of various properties of a file
File Collection	Contains a set of file objects and is stored as a property of another object, such as a Folder
FileSystemObject	Used to gain access to a computer's file system
Folder	Allows access and handling of various properties of a folder
Folders Collection	The SubFolder property of a Folder object returns a Folders Collection of all the sub-folders in that folder

Match	Used to access the three read-only properties associated with the results of a search operation that uses a regular expression
Matches Collection	A collection of objects that contains the results of a search and match operation that uses a regular expression
RegExp	Used to look for and match all occurrences of a search string pattern inside a target string
TextStream	Provides sequential access to the contents of any file where the contents are in text-readable form

Constants

Color Constants	Constants can be: VBBlack, VBRed, VBGreen, VBYellow, VBBlue, VBMagenta, VBCyan, VBWhite
Comparison Constants	Constants can be: VBBinaryCompare, VBTextCompare, VBDataBaseCompare
Data Format Constants	Constants can be: VBGenerateDate, VBLongDate, VBShortDate, VBLongTime, VBShortTime

Date And Time Constants	Constants can be: VBSunday, VBMonday, etc.
File Attribute Constants	Used with the File.Attributes property. Constants can be: Normal, ReadOnly, Hidden, System, Volume, Directory, Archive, Alias, Compressed
File Input/Output Constants	Constants can be: ForReading, ForWriting, ForAppending
MsgBox	Constants can be: VBOKOnly, VBOKCancel, VBAbortRetryIgnore, VBYesNoCancel,VBYesNo, VBRetryCancel, VBCritical, VBQuestion, VBExclamation
VBObjectError Constant	Constant can be: VBCR (Carriage return), VBCrLf (Carriage return & line feed), VBFormFeed, VBLF (Line feed), VBNewLine, VBNullChar, VBNullString, VBTab, VBVerticalTab
Tristate Constants	Constants can be: TristateTrue (-1), TristateFalse (0), TristateDefault (-2)
VarType Constants	Constants can be: VBEmpty, VBNull, VBInteger, VBLong, VBSingle, VBDouble, VBCurrency, VBDate, VBString, VBObject, VBError, VBBoolean, VBVariant, VBDataObject, VBDecimal, VBByte, VBArray

13

Glossary of Terms

Access control | A security mechanism that determines which operations a user is authorised to perform on a PC, a file, a printer, etc.

Active partition | A partition from which an x86-based computer starts up. The active partition must be a primary partition on a basic disc.

Add-in | A mini-program which runs in conjunction with another and enhances its functionality.

Address | A unique number or name that identifies a specific computer or user on a network.

Administrator | For Windows XP Professional, a person responsible for setting up and managing local computers, their user and group accounts, and assigning passwords and permissions.

Anonymous FTP | Anonymous FTP allows you to connect to a remote computer and transfer public files back to your local computer without the need to have a user ID and password.

ANSI | American National Standards Institute. A US government organisation responsible for improving communication standards.

Applet	A program that can be downloaded over a network and launched on the user's computer.
ASCII	A binary code representation of a character set. The name stands for 'American Standard Code for Information Interchange'.
ASP	Active Server Page. File format used for dynamic Web pages that get their data from a server based database.
Association	An identification of a filename extension to a program. This lets Windows open the program when its files are selected.
Authoring	The process of creating web documents or software.
Backup	To make a back-up copy of a file or a disc for safekeeping.
Bandwidth	The range of transmission frequencies a network can use. The greater the bandwidth the more information that can be transferred over a network.
Basic volume	A primary partition or logical drive that resides on a basic disc.
Batch file	A file that contains commands which are automatically executed when the file is run.
Baud rate	The speed at which a modem communicates.
Binary	A base-2 number system in which values are expressed as combinations of two digits, 0 and 1.
Bit	The smallest unit of information handled by a computer.

Boot partition	The partition on a hard disc that contains the operating system and its support files.
Boot up	To start your computer by switching it on, which initiates a self test of its Random Access Memory (RAM), then loads the necessary system files.
Broadband	A communications systems in which the medium of transmission (such as a wire or fibre-optic cable) carries multiple messages at a time.
Broadcast	An address that is destined for all hosts on a particular network segment.
Browse	A button in some Windows dialogue boxes that lets you view a list of files and folders before you make a selection. Also to view a Web page.
Browser	A program, like the Internet Explorer, that lets you view Web pages.
Bug	An error in coding or logic that causes a program to malfunction.
Bytes	A unit of data that holds a single character, such as a letter, a digit.
Cable modem	A device that enables a broadband connection to the Internet by using cable television infrastructure.
Cache	An area of memory, or disc space, reserved for data, which speeds up downloading.
CD-R	Recordable compact disc.
CD-ROM	Compact Disc - Read Only Memory; an optical disc which information may be read from but not written to.

CD-RW	Rewritable compact disc. Data can be copied to the CD on more than one occasion and can be erased.
Cgi-bin	The most common name of a directory on a web server in which CGI programs are stored.
Client	A computer that has access to services over a computer network. The computer providing the services is a server.
Client application	A Windows application that can accept linked, or embedded, objects.
Clipboard	A temporary storage area of memory, where text and graphics are stored with the cut and copy actions. The Office XP clipboard can store up to 24 items.
Command	An instruction given to a computer to carry out a particular action.
Command prompt	A window used to interface with the MS-DOS operating system.
Compressed file	One that is compacted to save server space and reduce transfer times. Typical file extension for DOS/Windows is .zip.
Configuration	A general purpose term referring to the way you have your computer set up.
Cookies	Files stored on your hard drive by your Web browser that hold information for it to use.
Data packet	A unit of information transmitted as a whole from one device to another on a network.
Default	The command, device or option automatically chosen.

Defragmentation	The process of rewriting parts of a file to contiguous sectors on a hard disc to increase the speed of access and retrieval.
Desktop	The Windows screen working background.
Device driver	A special file that must be loaded into memory for Windows to be able to address a specific procedure or hardware device.
Device name	A logical name used by an operating system to identify a device, such as LPT1 or COM1 for the parallel or serial printer.
Dial-up Connection	A popular form of Net connection for the home user, over standard telephone lines.
Digital signature	A means for originators of a message, file, or other digitally encoded information to bind their identity to the information.
Direct Connection	A permanent connection between your computer system and the Internet.
Directory	An area on disc where information relating to a group of files is kept. Also known as a folder.
Disc	A device on which you can store programs and data.
Disconnect	To detach a drive, port or computer from a shared device, or to break an Internet connection.
Display adapter	An expansion board that plugs into a PC to give it display capabilities.
DLL	Dynamic Link Library; An OS feature that allows files with the .dll extensions

	to be loaded only when needed by the program.
Document	A file produced by an application program. When used in reference to the Web, a document is any file containing text, media or hyperlinks that can be transferred from an HTTP server to a browser.
Domain	A group of devices, servers and computers on a network.
Double-click	To quickly press and release a mouse button twice.
Download	To transfer to your computer a file, or data, from another computer.
DPI	Dots Per Inch - a resolution standard for laser printers.
Drag	To move an object on the screen by pressing and holding down the left mouse button while moving the mouse.
Drive name	The letter followed by a colon which identifies a floppy or hard disc drive.
DSL	Digital Subscriber Line - a broad-band connection to the Internet through existing copper telephone wires.
Dual boot	A PC configuration that can start two different operating systems.
DVD	Digital Video Disc; a type of optical disc technology. It looks like a CD but can store greater amounts of data.
Encrypted password	A password that is scrambled.
Engine	Software used by search services.
Ethernet	A very common method of networking computers in a LAN.

Extract a file | Create an uncompressed copy of the file in a folder you specify.

FAT | The File Allocation Table. An area on disc where information is kept on which part of the disc a file is located.

File extension | The suffix following the period in a filename. Windows uses this to identify the source application program. For example **.mdb** indicates a Microsoft Access file.

Filter | A set of criteria that is applied to data to show a subset of the data.

Firewall | Security measures designed to protect a networked system from unauthorised access.

Floppy disc | A removable disc on which information can be stored magnetically.

Folder | An area used to store a group of files, usually with a common link.

Font | A graphic design representing a set of characters, numbers and symbols.

Fragmentation | The scattering of parts of the same file over different areas of the disc.

Freeware | Software that is available for downloading and unlimited use without charge.

FTP | File Transfer Protocol. The procedure for connecting to a remote computer and transferring files.

Function key | One of the series of 10 or 12 keys marked with the letter F and a numeral, used for specific operations.

Gateway	A computer system that allows otherwise incompatible networks to communicate with each other.
GIF	Graphics Interchange Format, a common standard for images on the Web.
Gigabyte	(GB); 1,024 megabytes. Usually thought of as one billion bytes.
Graphic	A picture or illustration, also called an image. Formats include GIF, JPEG, BMP, PCX, and TIFF.
Group	A collection of users, computers, contacts, and other groups.
Handshaking	A series of signals acknowledging that communication can take place between computers or other devices.
Hard copy	Output on paper.
Hardware	The equipment that makes up a computer system, excluding the programs or software.
Helper application	A program allowing you to view multimedia files that your web browser cannot handle internally.
Hibernation	A state in which your computer shuts down after saving everything in memory on your hard disc.
Home page	The document displayed when you first open your Web browser, or the first document you come to at a Web site.
Host	Computer connected directly to the Internet that provides services to other local and/or remote computers.

HTML	HyperText Markup Language, the format used in documents on the Web.
HTML editor	Authoring tool which assists with the creation of HTML pages.
HTTP	HyperText Transport Protocol, the system used to link and transfer hypertext documents on the Web.
Hub	A common connection point for devices in a network.
Hyperlink	A segment of text, or an image, that refers to another document on the Web, an Intranet or your PC.
Hypertext	A system that allows documents to be cross-linked so that the reader can explore related links, or documents, by clicking on a highlighted symbol.
Interface	A device that allows you to connect a computer to its peripherals.
Internet	The global system of computer networks.
Intranet	A private network inside an organisation using the same kind of software as the Internet.
IP	Internet Protocol - The rules that provide basic Internet functions.
IP Address	Internet Protocol Address - every computer on the Internet has a unique identifying number.
ISDN	Integrated Services Digital Network, a telecom standard using digital transmission technology to support voice, video and data communications applications over regular telephone lines.

ISP	Internet Service Provider - A company that offers access to the Internet.
Java	An object-oriented programming language created by Sun Microsystems for developing applications and applets that are capable of running on any computer, regardless of the operating system.
Kernel	The core of layered architecture that manages the most basic operations of the operating system and the computer's processor.
Kilobyte	(KB); 1024 bytes of information or storage space.
LAN	Local Area Network - High-speed, privately-owned network covering a limited geographical area, such as an office or a building.
Linked object	An object that is inserted into a document but still exists in the source file. Changing the original object automatically updates it within the linked document.
Links	The hypertext connections between Web pages.
Local	A resource that is located on your computer, not linked to it over a network.
Location	An Internet address.
Log on	To gain access to a network.
Megabyte	(MB); 1024 kilobytes of information or storage space.
Megahertz	(MHz); Speed of processor in millions of cycles per second.

Memory	Part of computer consisting of storage elements organised into addressable locations that can hold data and instructions.
MIME	Multipurpose Internet Mail Extensions, a messaging standard that allows Internet users to exchange e-mail messages enhanced with graphics, video and voice.
MIPS	Million Instructions Per Second; measures speed of a system.
Modem	Short for Modulator-demodulator devices. An electronic device that lets computers communicate electronically.
MS-DOS	Microsoft's implementation of the Disc Operating System for PCs.
Multitasking	Performing more than one operation at the same time.
Network	Two or more computers connected together to share resources.
Network adapter	A device that connects your computer to a network.
Network server	Central computer which stores files for several linked computers.
Node	Any single computer connected to a network.
NTFS file system	An advanced file system that provides performance, security, reliability, and advanced features that are not found in any version of FAT.
Online	Having access to the Internet.
Page	An HTML document, or Web site.

Parallel port	The input/output connector for a parallel interface device. Printers are generally plugged into a parallel port.
Partition	A portion of a physical disc that functions as though it were a physically separate disc.
PATH	The location of a file in the directory tree.
Peripheral	Any device attached to a PC.
Pixel	A picture element on screen; the smallest element that can be independently assigned colour and intensity.
Plug-and-play	Hardware which can be plugged into a PC and be used immediately without configuration.
POP3	Post Office Protocol - a method of storing and returning e-mail.
Port	The place where information goes into or out of a computer, e.g. a modem might be connected to the serial port.
PostScript	A page-description language (PDL), developed by Adobe Systems for printing on laser printers.
PPP	Point-to-Point Protocol - One of two methods (see SLIP) for using special software to establish a temporary direct connection to the Internet over regular phone lines.
Print queue	A list of print jobs waiting to be sent to a printer.
Program	A set of instructions which cause a computer to perform tasks.

Protocol	A set of rules or standards that define how computers communicate with each other.
Queue	A list of e-mail messages waiting to be sent over the Internet.
RAM	Random Access Memory. The computer's volatile memory. Data held in it is lost when power is switched off.
Real mode	MS-DOS mode, typically used to run programs, such as MS-DOS games, that will not run under Windows.
Refresh	To update displayed information with current data.
Registered file type	File types that are tracked by the system registry and are recognised by the programs you have installed on your computer.
Registry	A database where information about a computer's configuration is deposited. The registry contains information that Windows continually references during its operation.
Remote computer	A computer that you can access only by using a communications line or a communications device, such as a network card or a modem.
Resource	A directory, or printer, that can be shared over a network.
Robot	A Web agent that visits sites, by requesting documents from them, for the purposes of indexing for search engines. Also known as Wanderers, Crawlers, or Spiders.
ROM	Read Only Memory. A PC's non-volatile memory. Data is written into this

	memory at manufacture and is not affected by power loss.
Root	The highest or uppermost level in a hierarchically organised disc directory.
RTF	Rich Text Format. An enhanced form of text that includes basic formatting and is used for transferring data between applications, or in e-mail messages.
Script	A type of program consisting of a set of instructions to an application or tool program.
Search	Submit a query to a search engine.
Search engine	A program that helps users find information across the Internet.
Server	A computer system that manages and delivers information for client computers.
Shared resource	Any device, program or file that is available to network users.
Shareware	Software that is available on public networks and bulletin boards. Users are expected to pay a nominal amount to the software developer.
Signature file	An ASCII text file, maintained within e-mail programs, that contains text for your signature.
Site	A place on the Internet. Every Web page has a location where it resides which is called its site.
SMTP	Simple Mail Transfer Protocol - a protocol dictating how e-mail messages are exchanged over the Internet.

Spooler	Software which handles transfer of information to a store to be used by a peripheral device.
Standby	A state in which your computer consumes less power when it is idle, but remains available for immediate use.
System disc	A disc containing files to enable a PC to start up.
System files	Files used by Windows to load, configure, and run the operating system.
Task Manager	A utility that provides information about programs and processes running on the computer. Using Task Manager, you can end or run programs and end processes, and display a dynamic overview of your computer's performance.
Task Pane	A pane or sub-window that gives a range of options pertaining to the task currently being performed. New to Office XP applications.
TCP/IP	Transmission Control Protocol/ Internet Protocol, combined protocols that perform the transfer of data between two computers. TCP monitors and ensures the correct transfer of data. IP receives the data, breaks it up into packets, and sends it to a network within the Internet.
Text file	An unformatted file of text characters saved in ASCII format.
Toggle	To turn an action on and off with the same switch.

Uninstall	When referring to software, the act of removing program files and folders from your hard disc and removing related data from your registry so the software is no longer available.
Upload/Download	The process of transferring files between computers. Files are uploaded from your computer to another and downloaded from another computer to your own.
URL	Uniform Resource Locator, the addressing system used on the Web, containing information about the method of access, the server to be accessed and the path of the file to be accessed.
USB	Universal Serial Bus - an external bus standard that enables data transfer rates of 12 Mbps.
Usenet	Informal network of computers that allow the posting and reading of messages in newsgroups that focus on specific topics.
User ID	The unique identifier, usually used in conjunction with a password, which identifies you on a computer.
Virus	A malicious program, downloaded from a web site or disc, designed to wipe out information on your computer.
Volume	An area of storage on a hard disc. A volume is formatted by using a file system, such as FAT or NTFS, and has a drive letter assigned to it.
WINSOCK	A Microsoft Windows file that provides the interface to TCP/IP services.

Index

Companion Discs

COMPANION DISCS are available for most computer books written by the same author(s) and published by BERNARD BABANI (publishing) LTD, as listed at the front of this book (except for those marked with an asterisk). These books contain many pages of file/program listings.

There is no Companion Disc for this book.

To obtain companion discs for other books, fill in the order form below, or a copy of it, enclose a cheque (payable to **P.R.M. Oliver**) or a postal order, and send it to the address given below. **Make sure you fill in your name and address** and specify the book number and title in your order.

Book No.	Book Name	Unit Price	Total Price
BP		£3.50	
BP		£3.50	
BP		£3.50	
Name .... Address		Sub-total	£............
		P & P (@ 45p/disc)	£............
		Total Due	£............

Send to: P.R.M. Oliver, West Trevarth House, West Trevarth, Nr Redruth, Cornwall, TR16 5TJ